WEBSTER'S
NEW

STYLE GUIDE

Edited by John A. Haslem, Jr.

CONTENTS

Foreword

With this style guide on your desk, you'll never again be puzzled by such questions as

• Does this sentence need a comma or a semicolon?
• Does *XYZ Corporation* need a singular or plural verb?
• What is the difference between *abbreviate* and *abridge*? *allege* and *claim*? *farther* and *further*?
• Which compound words need a hyphen and which do not?
• Are abbreviations acceptable in a letter or report?
• Is it *differ from* or *differ with* in this sentence?

The *Webster's New Style Guide* answers all these questions and many, many more. It includes a concise review of English grammar, and of the basic rules of punctuation. The usage section illustrates the correct use of terms that are often confused or misused. The rules for compound words are accompanied by hundreds of examples of commonly used business and technical terms. There is a complete review of the rules of capitalization, a section on the uses of numerals in formal writing, and alphabetical lists of standard abbreviations with definitions for each entry. And for writers of letters there are useful tables indicating correct forms of address. This conveniently sized reference is packed with all the information you need to do your job quickly, easily, and correctly.

GRAMMAR

This section provides a brief review of English grammar, concentrating on common errors.

PARTS OF SPEECH

Noun

A noun is a word used to name a person, place, idea, thing, or quality.

>   Shakespeare, Paris, desk, truth

Pronoun

A pronoun is a word used in place of a noun.

>   I, we, who, these, each, himself

Verb

A verb is a word or group of words that denotes action, occurrence, or state of being. The verb, together with any words that complete or modify its meaning, forms the predicate of the sentence.

>   am, has washed, ran, will be seen

Adjective

An adjective is a word that describes or limits (modifies) the meaning of a noun or pronoun.

> *higher* morale, *net* income, *rolling* stone

Adverb

An adverb is a word that modifies a verb, an adjective, or another adverb. It answers the questions where, how or how much, or when.

> write *legibly*, long *enough*, *very* high production, do it *soon*, go *there*

Preposition

A preposition is a word used to relate a noun or pronoun to some other word in the sentence.

> at, in, by, from, toward

Conjunction

A conjunction is a word used to join words, phrases, or clauses.

> and, but, nor, since, although, when

Interjection

An interjection is an exclamation that expresses strong feeling.

Ah! Nonsense! Shh! Bravo!

Note that the part of speech (grammatical function) represented by a given word is determined by its use in a sentence. For instance, *but* may be an adverb, a preposition, or a conjunction, depending on how it is used.

PHRASES AND CLAUSES

Phrases and clauses are groups of grammatically related words that function as a single part of speech (*noun, adjective,* or *adverb*) or as a sentence.

Phrase

A phrase is a group of grammatically related words *without a subject, a predicate, or both.* A phrase is used as a *noun, adjective,* or *adverb.* Phrases are classified as:

Prepositional:	Put the finished letter *in the mail.* (also adverbial phrase)
	The man *in the red swimsuit* is looking for attention. (also adjective phrase)
Participial:	The woman *giving the talk* speaks with conviction. (also adjective phrase)

Gerund:	*Skiing deep powder* is both exciting and challenging. (also noun phrase)
Infinitive:	Our purpose is *to eat as inexpensively as we can.* (also noun phrase)
	The teacher assigned work *to be done quickly.* (also adjective phrase)
	She ran *to catch the horse.* (also adverbial phrase)

Clause

A clause is a group of grammatically related words containing both a subject and a predicate.

Independent (or main) clauses make a complete statement and are not introduced by any subordinating word. When it stands alone, it is a simple sentence.

We will return the favor.

Dependent (or subordinate) clauses cannot stand alone as simple sentences, usually because they are introduced by a subordinating word. Dependent clauses are classified as:

Adjective:	This is the man *who wrote to us for information.*

I have the video *he is looking for.* ("that" understood)

Adverb: *As soon as you have finished icing the cake*, bring it to the table.

Noun: *Whoever conducts the meeting* will be able to answer your questions.

Can you tell me *what my charges will total?*

TYPES OF SENTENCES

Simple Sentence

A simple sentence contains only one independent clause. This does not mean, however, that it must be short. It may include many phrases, a compound subject or predicate, and/or a number of modifiers.

The prisoner escaped.

You should run to the store next door and buy as many tortillas as you can.

Compound Sentence

A compound sentence contains two or more independent clauses, each of which could be written as a simple sentence.

You may want to vacation in the Bahamas, or you may prefer Acapulco instead.

Complex Sentence

A complex sentence contains one independent clause and one or more dependent clauses.

Since the freeway was jammed, we looked for an alternate route.

Compound-Complex Sentence

A compound-complex sentence contains two or more independent clauses and one or more dependent clauses.

Since they moved to town, the river flooded three times, and the stores all shut down.

PARTS OF A SENTENCE

The basic parts of a sentence are the *subject, verb,* and *complement. Modifiers* and *connectives* support this basic sentence structure—modifiers by making the meaning more exact and connectives by showing the relationship between parts.

Subject

The subject of a sentence is the word or group of words that names the thing, person, place, or idea about which a sentence makes a statement. These words or groups of words can include *nouns; pronouns; gerunds; infinitives; demonstrative, interrogative,* and *indefinite pronouns; phrases;* and *clauses.*

Nouns and **pronouns** are the single words most often used as subjects.

> The *director* called the meeting for 3 o'clock. (noun)

> *He* wants everybody to attend. (personal pronoun)

Gerunds and, less often, **infinitives,** are two verbals that may also be the subject of a sentence.

> *Walking* is good exercise. (gerund)

> *To run* is more tiring than to walk. (infinitive)

Demonstrative, interrogative, and **indefinite pronouns** are among the other parts of speech used as subjects.

> *That* is going to be a difficult task. (demonstrative)

> *What* are your plans for doing it? (interrogative)

> *Everyone* is eager to have you succeed. (indefinite)

Phrases serving as a noun may be the subject of a sentence.

Adopting that kitten was the smartest thing he did.

To learn as many languages as possible is his objective.

Clauses in their entirety may be used as the subject.

Whoever answers the telephone will get a chance to win the prize.

Whether the wild burro has been released or not will determine our action.

Verb

The verb tells what the subject itself does, what something else does to the subject, or what the subject is. Verbals, although they come from verbs, cannot serve as verbs in the predicate of a sentence. (For more on verbs and verbals, see the comprehensive section that follows.)

There are three types of verbs: *transitive verbs; intransitive verbs;* and *copulative* or *linking verbs*.

Transitive verbs take a direct object.

He *hit* the ball.

Intransitive verbs take no direct object.

She *fell* down.

Copulative or **linking verbs** take a predicate noun or predicate adjective.

> Jim *is* captain.

> Jim *seems* strong.

The properties of a verb are *number, person, tense, mood,* and *voice.* To indicate these properties we either change the form of the verb itself or add other verb forms called *auxiliary verbs—be, have, can, may, might, shall, will, should, would, could, must, do.*

Number tells whether the verb is singular or plural.

Person tells whether the first person (*I*), second person (*you*), or third person (*he, it, she*) is performing the action. A verb and its subject must agree in number and person. (This problem of agreement—so essential to the writing of clear sentences—is discussed in the section on Agreement and Reference.)

Tense is the means by which we show the time of an action—whether it happened in the past, is happening in the present, or will happen in the future.

Mood (indicative, imperative, subjunctive) indicates the manner of assertion—statement, command, wish, or condition.

Voice is the property of a verb that indicates whether the subject is performing or receiving the action of the verb. A verb in the *active voice* tells what the subject is doing; a verb in the *passive voice* tells what is being done to the subject.

> The *athlete completed* his training on time. (The verb *completed*, in the active voice, tells what the subject, *athlete*, did.)

> The *cereal was dropped* on the floor. (The verb *was dropped*, in the passive voice, tells what was done to the subject, *cereal*.)

Complement

The complement is the word or group of words that follows the verb and completes its meaning. A complement may be a *direct object*, an *indirect object*, a *predicate nominative*, a *predicate adjective*.

Direct objects are nouns or other parts of speech functioning as nouns that receive the action of the verb.

> He gave the *map* to the tourist. (*Map* is the direct object of the verb.)

> We are trying *to launch a probe to Jupiter.* (The infinitive phrase is the direct object of the verb.)

> Give me *whatever information you have.* (The noun clause is the direct object of the verb.)

Indirect objects are nouns or other parts of speech functioning as nouns that indicate to whom (what) or for whom (what) the action of the verb is done.

He gave [to] *her* the tickets. (*Her* is the indirect object of the verb; *tickets* is the direct object.)

Give [to] *whoever answers the door* the bouquet of flowers. (The noun clause is the indirect object of the verb.)

David did [for] *Jerry* a big favor. (*Jerry* is the indirect object; *favor* is the direct object.)

Predicate nominatives are also called predicate nouns, predicate complements, or subjective complements. The predicate nominative follows copulative, or linking, verbs and renames the subject. It can be a noun, a pronoun, a verbal, a phrase, or a clause.

Noun:	He is *chairman* of the committee.
Pronoun:	They thought the author was *she.*
Gerund:	My favorite exercise is *swimming.*
Infinitive phrase:	The purpose of this experiment is *to test the new engine.*
Noun clause:	The next president should be *whoever is best qualified.*

Predicate adjectives are adjectives (or adjective phrases) appearing in the predicate that modify the subject. A predicate adjective occurs only after copulative, or linking, verbs.

> The flower smells *sweet*.

> The meeting we are planning for Tuesday will be *on that subject*.

> This material is *over my head*.

> He appears *enthusiastic* about learning to dance.

Modifiers

Modifiers are single words, phrases, or clauses used to limit, describe, or define some element of the sentence. These are classed as either *adjectives* or *adverbs*. A modifier is said to "dangle" when it cannot attach both logically and grammatically to a specific element in the sentence. (For more on modifiers and modification, see the comprehensive section that follows.)

Adjectives describe or limit the meaning of nouns or pronouns.

> The *wily* raccoon was caught in the *baited* trap and transported to an *animal* shelter for *medical* tests.

The statistics *on juvenile crime* are alarming. (prepositional phrase used as an adjective)

The report *submitted by the audit committee* is being studied. (participial phrase used as an adjective)

Adverbs modify verbs, verbals, adjectives, or other adverbs. They answer the questions where, how or how much, when, and why?

We will hold the meeting *here*. (Where?)

The car accelerated *rapidly*. (How?)

Spending *excessively,* he ran out of funds. (How much?)

Let's eat the lasagna *as soon as it is finished cooking*. (When?)

Pete went downtown *to buy a tie*. (Why?)

Connectives

Connectives join one part of a sentence with another and show the relationship between the parts they connect. Connectives joining elements of equal rank include: *coordinate conjunctions, correlative conjunctions,* and *conjunctive adverbs*. Connectives joining elements of unequal rank include: *subordinate conjunctions, relative pronouns,* and *relative adverbs*. *Prepositions* are also some of the most important connectives. (For more on the usage of these and other connectives, see the Connectives section.)

Coordinate conjunctions are perhaps the most frequently used connectives. They join sentence elements of equal grammatical importance—words with words, phrases with phrases, independent clauses with independent clauses. The commonly used coordinate conjunctions are:

> *and, but, or, nor, for, yet*

Correlative conjunctions work in pairs to connect sentence elements of equal rank. Each member of a pair of correlative conjunctions must be followed by the same part of speech. Examples of these conjunctions are:

> *either . . . or, neither . . . nor, not only . . . but also, both . . . and*

Conjunctive adverbs connect independent clauses and show a relation of equal rank between them. Although the clause introduced by the conjunctive adverb is *grammatically* independent, it is *logically* dependent upon the preceding clause for its complete meaning. These are some conjunctive adverbs:

> *therefore, however, consequently, accordingly, furthermore, moreover, nevertheless*

Subordinate conjunctions introduce dependent adverb clauses and join them to independent clauses. Some of these conjunctions are:

> *before, since, after, as, because, if, unless, until, although*

> **NOTE:** The subordinate conjunction *that* introduces a noun clause:
>
> When he calls, tell him that *I had to leave for a meeting.*

Relative pronouns not only introduce noun and adjective clauses but also act as pronouns within their own clauses. These pronouns include:

> *that, which, who, whom, whatever, whichever, whoever*

> The salesperson *who called for an appointment* has just arrived. (adjective clause)

> Tell me the news *that you just heard.* (noun clause)

Relative adverbs introduce subordinate clauses. The most common of these connectives are:

> *how, where, when, while*

Prepositions show the relationship between a word that follows them, called the object, and a word before them to which they relate. Some prepositions are:

> *to, of, by, from, between, in, over, under, for*

Verbals

Verbals are nonfinite verbs used as a noun, an adjective, or an adverb. A nonfinite verb can never stand as the only verb in a sentence. There are three verbal forms: *infinitives, participles, gerunds*. (For more on verbs and verbals, see the Verbs and Verbals section that follows.)

Infinitives (to go, to run, to see, etc.) may act as a noun *or* an adjective *or* an adverb.

> I like *to swim*. (noun)

> A book *to read* is what she wants. (adjective)

> He went *to play* golf. (adverb)

Participles may be either a present participle (going, seeing, feeling, etc.) or a past participle (having gone, having seen, having felt, etc.). A participle acts *only* as an adjective.

> *Going* to the store, Jamal slipped. (adjective)

> *Having seen* the entire movie, Judy left the theater. (adjective)

Gerunds (knowing, running, hearing, etc.) act *only* as nouns.

> Charlie enjoys *running*. (noun)
>
> *Dancing* is a good way to enjoy music. (noun)

NOUNS AND PRONOUNS

A noun names a person, thing, idea, place, or quality. There are five classes of nouns: *proper, common, collective, concrete,* and *abstract.*

Pronouns stand in place of nouns. The six classes of pronouns are: *personal, relative, interrogative, indefinite, demonstrative,* and *reflexive.*

Proper Nouns

A proper noun names a particular place, person, or thing. The writer's chief problem with proper nouns is recognizing them in order to capitalize them.

> Atlanta, Mr. Jones, the Commissioner of Education, Form 1040

Common Nouns

A common noun names a member of a class or group of persons, places, or things.

> hope, banana, education, form

Collective Nouns

A collective noun, singular in form, names a group or collection of individuals. The chief problem with collective nouns is determining the number of the verb to use with the collective noun. For this reason, it is discussed at length in the section on agreement and reference.

>   committee, jury, council, task force

Concrete Nouns

A concrete noun names a particular or specific member of a class or group.

>   apple, *not* fruit; chair, *not* furniture

Abstract Nouns

An abstract noun names a quality, state, or idea.

>   beauty, truth, objectivity

Notice that common nouns can be concrete or abstract.

Personal Pronouns

The personal pronoun shows which person (first, second, or third) is the subject. Personal pronouns are troublesome because of their many forms; they change form to indicate number, person, and case.

The personal pronouns are:

> I, my, mine, me, you, your, yours, he, his, him, she, her, hers, it, and its, *and their plurals*—we, you, they, it, our, ours, your, yours, their, theirs, us, and them

Relative Pronouns

The relative pronoun serves two purposes: (1) it takes the place of a noun in the clause it introduces, and (2) like a conjunction, it connects its clause with the rest of the sentence.

The relative pronouns are:

> who, whom, which, that, what, whoever, whomever, whichever, whatever

The relative pronoun has the same number, person, and case as its antecedent.

Interrogative Pronouns

The interrogative pronoun is the same in form as the relative pronoun, but different in function. The interrogative pronoun asks a question.

who	
whom	refer to persons
what	refers to things
which	refers to person or things

As an adjective, *which* and *what* may be used.

> . . . which book? . . . what time?

Indefinite Pronouns

The indefinite pronouns listed here are singular, as are most indefinites:

> another, anyone, each, either, everyone, no one, nothing . . .

Demonstrative Pronouns

The demonstrative pronouns (*this, that, these, those*) point out or refer to a substantive (usually a noun) which has been clearly expressed or just as clearly implied. They may be used as pronouns

> *These* are the letters he wants.

or as adjectives

> Bring me *those* letters.

Reflexive Pronouns

The reflexive pronouns are compound personal pronouns:

> myself, yourself, yourselves, himself, themselves, ourselves, herself, itself

A reflexive pronoun emphasizes or intensifies a meaning. It is not set off by commas.

I *myself* will see that it is done.

The director *himself* gave the order.

You will take it to her *yourself.*

A reflexive pronoun often appears as the direct object of a verb; its antecedent, as the subject of the verb.

I taught *myself* how to type.

He hurt *himself* when he fell.

It can, however, be the object of a preposition,

He finished the job by *himself.*

He was beside *himself* with joy.

the indirect object of a verb,

I bought *myself* a new suit yesterday.

They gave *themselves* a pat on the back.

or a predicate nominative.

I am just not *myself* today.

They just were not *themselves* at the party.

In formal usage, the reflexive pronoun is not used where the shorter personal pronoun can be substituted for it with no change in meaning.

Not: Both the director and *myself* endorse the policy.

But: Both the director and I endorse the policy.

Avoid the following pronoun errors:

The use of *hisself* for *himself.*

The use of *theirselves* for *themselves.*

The use of *myself* or *yourself* instead of the personal pronoun *me, I,* or *you* in such constructions as "The secretary and *myself* opened the mail. It's ideal for a professional person such as *yourself.*"

CASE

Case is the property of a noun or pronoun which shows, either by inflection (change in form) or by position, the relation of the word to other parts of the sentence.

English has three cases: *nominative, objective,* and *possessive.*

All nouns and a few pronouns keep the same form in the nominative and in the objective cases. Consequently, we must depend on the position of these words in the sentence to indicate their function. Since nouns don't change form to indicate nominative and objective case, our only real difficulty with them comes in the formation and use of the possessive case.

On the other hand, some pronouns are inflected (change form) in the nominative and objective cases, as well as in the possessive. Because of this, the case of pronouns causes us more trouble than does the case of nouns.

Nominative Case

The nominative (or subjective) case is used primarily to name the subject of a verb or the predicate complement after a copulative, or linking, verb (such as *seem, appear,* or any form of *be*).

Not: Either *she* or *me* will be responsible.

But: Either *she* or *I* will be responsible. (Either *she* will be . . . or *I* will be . . .)

NOTE: An appositive, which is a word or group of words standing next to another word and denoting the same person or thing, is always in the same case as its antecedent (the word to which it stands in apposition). Therefore, if the antecedent is in the nominative case, the appositive must also be in the nominative case. If the antecedent is in the objective case, the appositive is also in the objective case.

| Not: | The representatives, *John and me,* are to meet on Friday. |
| But: | The representatives, *John and I,* are to meet on Friday. (*John and I* are to meet. . . .) |

Subject of a Verb in a Main Clause

A noun or pronoun serving as the subject of a verb (except the subject of an infinitive) is in the nominative case.

> *I* was late for work this morning.

> *He* is planning to finish his pancakes this morning.

> Neither *she nor I* had heard of this before.

> The culprits, *she and I,* were reprimanded.

Subject of a Relative Clause

A relative pronoun (*who, whoever, which, whichever*) used as the subject of a clause is in the nominative case.

> Give the letter to *whoever* answers the door.

> You'll want to decide *whichever* is best.

The clause itself may be a subject or an object; however, the case of the relative pronoun depends upon its use *within the clause.*

Whoever is selected must board the plane immediately.

The pronoun *who* used as the subject of a verb is not affected by a parenthetical expression such as *I think, he believes, they say* intervening between the subject and the verb.

She is the person *who* I think is best qualified. (*Who* is the subject of the clause.)

We asked Susan, *who* we knew *had always been* a climber of mountains. (*Who* is the subject of the clause.)

Ms. Mann is the attorney *who* we suppose *will prepare* the brief. (*Who* is the subject of the clause.)

Subject of a Clause Introduced by *than* or *as*

If the word following *than* or *as* introduces a clause, even if part of the clause is understood, that word must be in the nominative case. But if the word following *than* or *as* does not introduce a clause, it must be in the objective case. To test whether the word should be in the nominative or objective case, complete the clause.

He has been here longer than *she*. (than *she has*)

Mary is a better mathematician than *I*. (than *I am*)

They were as late as *we* in filing our tax returns. (as *we were*)

We were seated as promptly as *they*. (as *they were*)

In the following examples, the word following *than* or *as* may be in either the nominative or the objective case, depending on the intended meaning. If there is any chance your meaning might be misunderstood, complete the clause.

She likes this work better than *I*. (than *I like it*)

She likes this work better than *me*. (than *she likes me*)

I have known John as long as *she*. (as *she has*)

I have known John as long as *her*. (as *I have known her*)

Words Following Forms of *be* (Predicate Nominative)

A noun or pronoun following a form of the verb *be* (except for the infinitive if it has its own subject) must be in the nominative case. (This word is called the *predicate nominative*—or, if a noun, the *predicate noun*.) The general rule applying to this construction is that the word following the verb *be* must be in the same case as the word before the verb.

Imagine that the verb *be* has the same meaning as the equals sign (=) in mathematics.

Not: They thought I was *him*.

But: They thought I was *he*. (*I = he*)

A noun or pronoun following the infinitive *to be* is in the nominative case if the infinitive has no subject.

He was thought to be *I*.

My brother was taken to be *I*.

NOTE: You may have trouble when one or both of the members of the compound subject or predicate nominative are pronouns. Try this simple test: decide which case would be appropriate if *one* pronoun were the simple subject or predicate nominative, and then use the same case for both.

Example:
The new *chairmen* are *he and I*.
Reverse positions:
He and I are the new *chairmen*.

Example:
If any one of the free agents is chosen, *it* should be *he*.
Reverse positions:
If any one of the free agents is chosen, *he* should be *it*.

> *Example:*
> The *author* was thought to be *I.*
> Reverse positions:
> *I* was thought to be the *author.*
>
> *These examples show the proper forms for formal use. In informal English, the objective case forms are often encountered.*

Direct Address

Direct address is a construction used parenthetically to direct spoken language to some particular person. Nouns or pronouns in direct address are in the nominative case and are set off by commas. This construction will cause little trouble, since proper names, which are the main examples of direct address, do not change form to indicate case.

Jim, come here for a minute.

It is true, *sir,* that I made that remark.

Tell me, *doctor,* is he showing much improvement?

Objective Case

The objective (or accusative) case is used chiefly to name the receiver or object of the action of a verb, or to name the object of a preposition.

When one part of a compound expression (joined by a coordinate conjunction) is in the objective case, all other parts of the same expression must also be in the objective case.

> When you reach the station call either *him* or *me*.

> The work was given to *you* and *me*.

When the antecedent of an appositive is in the objective case because it is serving a function that requires that case, the appositive must also be in the objective case.

> The teacher has appointed *us, you and me,* to the group.

> He gave *us passengers* a copy of the schedule.

> The principle is basic to *us Americans*.

Direct Object of a Verb or Verbal
A noun or pronoun serving as the direct object of a verb or verbal is in the objective case.

> The driver returned *him* to his home.

> My father called *him* and *me* to come back inside.

> They will invite *us fans* to the football game.

Whomever you called on Monday night is certainly upset.

but

Call *whoever* is responsible before the alarm sounds.

I enjoyed meeting *him.*

I didn't intend to ask *them* again.

Having called *him* and told *him* of our plan, we left for the evening.

We have a letter from her cousin thanking *us* for our courtesy.

Indirect Object of a Verb or Verbal
A word used as the indirect object of a verb or verbal is in the objective case.

The ballplayer gave *me* his autograph.

The supervisor assigned *him* and *me* the task of cleaning up the boardroom.

The inspector showed *us employees* the operation of the meat grinder.

A letter giving *him* authority to represent his mother is being prepared.

Object of a Preposition

A noun or pronoun serving as the object of a preposition is in the objective case.

> From *whom* did you receive the letter? (*Whom* is the object of the preposition *from.*)

> **NOTE:** *But* is a preposition when *except* may be substituted for it with no change in meaning.
>
> Everyone is going but *me.*

A special troublemaker is the compound object *you and me* after the preposition *between.* Do not say *between you and I;* say *between you and me.*

Subject of an Infinitive

A noun or pronoun used as the subject of an infinitive is in the objective case.

> I want *him* to have this car.

> We expect *him* to finish that job.

> They invited *her and me* to attend the reception.

> *Whom* will he cast to play the lead character?

Words Following Infinitive *to be*

The verb *to be* takes the same case after it as before it. Since the subject of an infinitive is in the objective case, a word following the infinitive is also in the objective case.

> They thought him to be *me*. (Reverse, to test choice of case: They thought *me* to be *him*.)

> We assumed the author of the letter to be *him*. (Reverse: We assumed *him* to be the *author*....)

> They did not expect the representatives to be *him and me*. (Reverse: They did not expect *him and me* to be the *representatives*.)

Subject of a Participle and of a Gerund

The subject of a participle is in the objective case. The problem comes in determining whether a verbal is a participle or a gerund. Both may have the same form (the *-ing* form of the verb), but only the subject of the *participle* is in the objective case. The subject of the *gerund* is in the possessive case.

> Imagine *him flying* an airplane. (The verbal *flying* is a participle modifying *him,* and the pronoun *him* is in the objective case.)

> Imagine *his flying* to Paris. (The verbal *flying* is a gerund, and the pronoun *his* is in the possessive case.)

> *His rushing* to catch the plane was in vain. (*Rushing* is a gerund, and its subject must be in the possessive case.)

We watched *him rushing* to catch the plane. (The verbal, *rushing,* is a participle modifying *him;* therefore, the subject, *him,* is in the objective case.)

> **NOTE:** In the gerund expression *its being,* the subject that follows must be in the objective case.
>
> In our search for the thief, we never thought of its being *him* (not *he*).

Possessive Case (and its Proper Punctuation)

The possessive (or genitive) case is used to indicate possession.

Possessive of Singular Words

To form the possessive of singular words not ending in *s* (including the indefinite pronouns), add the apostrophe and *s*.

the *student's* report; the *neighbor's* car; the *widow's* cat; *anyone's* guess; *somebody's* coat.

> **NOTE:** When *else* is used with an indefinite pronoun, form the possessive by adding the apostrophe and *s* to *else,* rather than to the indefinite pronoun.

somebody's coat	but: *somebody else's* coat
anyone's idea	but: *anyone else's* idea

To form the possessive of singular words ending in *s*, add the apostrophe and *s* or simply the apostrophe alone.

Singular form	*Possessive form*
boss	boss's or boss'
hostess	hostess's or hostess'

NOTE: The possessive of some proper names ending in *s*, however, is traditionally formed by adding only the apostrophe:

Jesus' disciples   Moses' staff

Some names of more than one syllable ending in *s*, as well as some ancient Greek names, also form the possessive in this way:

John Quincy Adams' presidency

Epimenides' paradox

The apostrophe is omitted in some organizational or geographical names that contain a possessive thought. Follow the form used by the organization itself.

Harpers Ferry
Pikes Peak

Governors Island
Citizens National Bank

Do not use the apostrophe in forming the possessive of the personal and relative pronouns. The possessive forms of these pronouns are:

Relative: whose

Personal: her, hers (*not* her's) his, their, theirs, our, ours, my, mine, your, yours, its

---

NOTE: *Its* is the possessive form of the personal pronoun *it*; *it's* is a contraction of *it is*. Similarly, *whose* is the possessive form of the relative pronoun *who*, and *who's* is a contraction of *who is* or *who has*. The examples below illustrate the correct use of these words.

Its operation is simple.
It's (*it is*) simple to operate.

Don't drive that car; *its* tires need changing.
Don't drive that car; *it's* in need of new tires.

Whose mailbox is that?
Who's (*who is*) going with me?

Theirs is in the closet.
There's very little time left.

Possessive of Plural Words

To form the possessive of a plural word not ending in *s,* add the apostrophe and *s.*

> men's, children's, women's, people's

To form the possessive of a plural word ending in *s,* add the apostrophe only.

> All of the *mechanics'* tools were lost.

NOTE: Avoid placing the apostrophe before the final *s* of a word if the *s* is actually a part of the singular or plural form. To test, first form the plural; then add the correct possessive sign.

> Not: ladie's   But: ladies'

> (*Ladies* is the plural form; since the word ends in *s,* add the apostrophe alone to form the possessive, *ladies'.*)

Use of the *of* Phrase to Form Possessive

Use the *of* phrase in forming the possessive to avoid the "piling up" of possessives.

Not: The *taxpayer's wife's income* must be reported.

But: The *income of the taxpayer's wife* must be reported.

Not: Her brother's friend's bicycle was red.

But: The bicycle of her brother's friend was red.

In order to avoid an awkward construction, use the *of* phrase to form the possessive of names consisting of several words.

Not: The local chapter of the National Association of Radio and Television Broadcasters' first meeting was held Thursday.

But: The first meeting of the local chapter of the National Association of Radio and Television Broadcasters was held Thursday.

Not: The Director of the Alcohol and Tobacco Tax Division's report . . .

But: The report of the Director of the Alcohol and Tobacco Tax Division . . .

Use the *of* phrase to avoid adding a possessive to a pronoun that is already possessive.

Not: We are going to a *friend of mine's* house.

But: We are going to the *house of a friend of mine.*

Possessive of Compound Words
Form the possessive on the last word of a compound word, whether or not the compound is hyphenated. A point to remember is that even though the plural

of a compound word is formed by adding *s* to the principal noun in the compound, the possessive is always formed by adding the sign of the possessive to the last word in the compound.

Singular	Singular Possessive
notary public	notary public's
comptroller general	comptroller general's
supervisor in charge	supervisor in charge's

Plural	Plural Possessive
notaries public	notaries public's
comptrollers general	comptrollers general's
supervisors in charge	supervisors in charge's

If a possessive is followed by an appositive or an explanatory phrase, form the possessive on the explanatory word.

> That was *Mr. Smith the auditor's* idea.

> I was acting on my *friend John's* advice.

> Have you read the *senator from Arizona's* speech?

If the appositive or explanatory words are set off by commas, the possessive may be found on both the main word and the explanatory word.

Either:	This is *Mary, my assistant's,* day off.
Or:	This is *Mary's, my assistant's,* day off.
Either:	I sent it to *Mr. Smith, the collector's,* office.
Or:	I sent it to *Mr. Smith's, the collector's,* office.

NOTE: The methods just illustrated are grammatically correct ways to show possession; they do, however, sound awkward. To be more effective (and just as correct), try using an *of* phrase to form the possessive of compound words.

Not:	This is the supervisor in charge's office.
But:	This is the office of the supervisor in charge.
Not:	I was acting on my friend John's advice.
But:	I was acting on the advice of my friend, John.
Not:	I sent it to Mr. Smith's, the collector's, office.
But:	I sent it to the office of Mr. Smith, the collector.

Joint, Separate, and Alternative Possession

When two or more people possess the same thing jointly, form the possessive on the last word only.

> She is *Mr. Smith and Ms. Henry's* cousin. (She is cousin to both people.)

> These pictures are from *John and Mary's* vacation trip.

> I bought my coat at *Woodward and Lothrop's.* (*store* understood)

NOTE: When one of the words involved in the joint possession is a pronoun, each word must be in the possessive.

> This is *John's, Bob's,* and *my* neighborhood.

> Have you seen *Mary's* and *his* new home?

When it is intended that each of the words in a series possess something individually, form the possessive on each word.

> *Barbara's* and *Mary's* singing are certainly different.

> The *drivers'* and the *owners'* associations are meeting here this week.

When alternative possession is intended, each word must be in the possessive.

I wouldn't want either *John's* or *Harry's* job.

Is that the *author's* or the *editor's* opinion?

Possessive of Abbreviations

Possessives of abbreviations are formed in the same way as are other possessives. Ordinarily the possessive sign is placed after the final period of the abbreviation where one is present.

Singular Possessive	Plural	Plural Possessive
MD's	MDs	MDs'
Dr.'s	Drs.	Drs.'

John Blank, *Jr.'s* account has been closed.
(Note that there is no comma after *Jr.* when the possessive is used.)

Parallel Possessives

Be sure that a word standing parallel with a possessive is itself possessive in form.

Not: *His* work, like an *accountant*, is exacting.

But: *His* work, like an *accountant's,* is exacting.

Not: The *agent's* job differs from the *auditor.*

But: The *agent's* job differs from the *auditor's.*

Not: *His* task is no more difficult than his *neighbor.*

But: *His* task is no more difficult than his *neighbor's.*

Possessive with a Gerund

A noun or pronoun immediately preceding a gerund is in the possessive case. A gerund is a verbal noun naming an action. A participle, which may have the same form as a gerund, functions as an adjective; its subject is in the objective case.

> *Our* being late delayed the meeting.

> *Mr. Jones's* being late delayed the meeting.

> You can always depend on *his* being a good friend.

> *Jim's* singing the anthem made all the difference.

> *Washington's* being the capital makes it different from other cities.

NOTE: There are two exceptions to this general rule:

Do not use the possessive case for the subject of a gerund unless the subject immediately precedes the gerund. If the subject and gerund are separated by other words, the subject must be in the objective case.

Not:	I can see no reason for a *man's* with his background *failing* to pass the test.

| But: | I can see no reason for a *man* with his background *failing* to pass the test. (Without intervening words: I can see no reason for a *man failing* to pass the test.) |

There are no possessive forms for the demonstrative pronouns *that, this, these,* and *those.* Therefore, when these words are used as subjects of a gerund they do not change form.

Not:	We cannot be sure of *that's* being true.
But:	We cannot be sure of *that* being true.
Not:	What are the chances of *this'* being sold?
But:	What are the chances of *this* being sold?

He/She

Traditionally, the personal pronoun *he* has been used in English when the gender of its antecedent is unknown.

Each child (boy or girl) develops at *his* own pace.

This usage is still widely accepted, but it is changing. If you prefer a more neutral form (he/she, for example), or if you think your reader may be offended, use instead a form of *he or she*.

Each child develops at *his or her* own pace.

Since the *he or she* form is somewhat clumsy, a frequent repetition of it may make your writing awkward. Avoid the problem by rewording.

All children develop at *their* own pace.

Take care to make pronouns and antecedents consistent within a passage.

AGREEMENT AND REFERENCE

Many grammatical errors result from failing to make different parts of a sentence agree in number, person, or gender.

The verb must agree with the subject in number and in person. If the subject is singular, the verb form must also be singular; if the subject is in the third person—*she, it, he*—the verb must be in the third person. The chief problem is identifying the true subject of the sentence and determining whether it is singular or plural.

The pronoun must agree with its antecedent (the word to which it refers—sometimes called its *referent*) in number, in person, and in gender. Of the three, gender causes the writer the least difficulty. The chief problem is identifying the antecedent and determining its number, person, and gender.

Often the subject of the verb is also the antecedent of the pronoun. You might think that this would greatly simplify things, and to some extent it does, for once you have determined that the subject-antecedent is singular, you know where you stand—both verb and pronoun must likewise be singular. A word of caution: be consistent. Don't shift from a singular verb (which properly agrees with its singular subject) to a plural pronoun later in the sentence.

Subject Problems

The first step in making the parts of a sentence agree is to identify the subject. In this section, therefore, we will discuss only those subjects that may present special problems.

Collective Words

A collective is a single word that names a group of people or things. Although usually singular in form, a collective is treated as either singular or plural according to the sense of the sentence.

A collective is treated as singular when members of the group act, or are considered, as a *unit*.

> The survey committee *is visiting* the district this week.

> The national office evaluation team *has* five trips scheduled for this quarter.

A collective is treated as plural when the members act, or are considered, *individually*.

> The jury *are* unable to agree on a verdict.

> The national office evaluation team *pool* the data *they* gather and *prepare their* report.

Common collectives include:

> assembly, association, audience, board, cabinet, class, commission, company, corporation, council, counsel, couple, crowd, department, family, firm, group, jury, majority, minority, number, pair, press, public, staff, United States

Company names also qualify as collectives and may be either singular or plural. Usually those ending with a plural signifier such as *s* are plural.

> Flowers, Inc., *mails its* advertisements in envelopes with floral decorations.

> Jones Brothers *have sent their* representative to the conference.

Short collectives include the following short words. Though seldom listed as collectives, these words are governed by the rule for collectives. They are singular or plural according to the intended meaning of the sentence.

all, any, more, most, none, some, who, which

When a prepositional phrase follows the short collective, the number of the noun in the phrase controls the number of the verb. When no such phrase follows, the writer signals the intended meaning by the choice of the singular or the plural verb.

Some of the *work has been done*.
Some of the *returns have been filed*.

Most of the *correspondence is* routine.
Most of the *letters are* acceptable.

Is there *any* left? (any portion—any money, any ink)
Are there *any* left? (any individual items—any forms, any copies)

Which is to be posted? (which one?)
Which are to be posted? (which ones?)

Either:	None of the items *is* deductible.
Or:	None of the items *are* deductible.

> **NOTE:** Many writers treat *none* as singular in every instance, since it is a compound of *no one.* This usage is correct. It is equally correct, however, to treat *none* as plural (meaning *not any*) when it is followed by a prepositional phrase that has a plural object. Those who want to emphasize the singular meaning often substitute *not one* for *none*:
>
>   *Not one* of the birds *is* building a nest.

Special collectives include certain words called *abstract collectives* by some grammarians. These words are also treated as collectives, even though they do not name a group of persons or things. Their singular form is used when they refer to qualities, emotions, or feelings common to a group of persons or things; or to actions common to such a group. Their plural form is used when this common or general idea is not present.

Use the singular under such circumstances as these:

attention	We called their *attention* to the plan's advantages. (not *attentions*)
consent	Several gave their *consent* to the guru.

failure	The dogs' *failure* to heed commands delayed their finding new homes.
interest	Their *interest* was in winning at all costs.
sense	Our interpretation is based on the *sense* of the amendment.
work	Rain will not interfere with their *work*.

Use either the singular or the plural with:

opinion	The students and their teacher expressed their *opinion* (or *opinions*) on the matter.
time	The only *time* these restrictions are in order *is* when the airlines . . . OR The only *times* these restrictions are in order *are* when the airlines . . .
use	What *use* (or *uses*) can be made of the timber?

Units of Measure

When a number is used with a plural noun to indicate a unit of measurement (money, time, fractions, portions, distance, weight, quantity, etc.), a singular verb is used. When the term is thought of as individual parts, a plural verb is used.

> *Ten years seems* like a long time.
> *Ten years have gone* by since I last saw him.

> *Twenty-one pages is* our homework for each day.
> *Twenty-one pages are* needed to finish the job.

When fractions and expressions such as *the rest of, the remainder of, a part of, percent of,* etc., are followed by a prepositional phrase, the noun or pronoun in that phrase governs the number of the verb.

> *Four-fifths* of the job *was* finished on time.
> *Four-fifths* of the students *were* finished on time.

> The *rest* (or *remainder*) of the work *is* due
> Friday.
> The *rest* (or *remainder*) of the cards *were*
> mailed today.

> What *percentage* of the information *is* available?
> What *percentage* of the items *were* lost?

Confusing Singular and Plural Forms

It is sometimes hard to tell by its form whether a word is singular or plural. Some words that end in -*s* may be singular, and some seemingly singular words may be plural.

These words are singular, though they may seem plural in form:

apparatus, news, summons, whereabouts

The *news* is disturbing.

These words are plural, though they are singular (or collective) in meaning:

assets, earnings, means (*income*), odds, premises, proceeds, quarters, savings, wages, winnings

His *assets are* listed on the attached statement.

Earnings are up this quarter.

The *odds are* against our getting home on time.

The *proceeds are* earmarked for the most needy.

These words may be either singular or plural, depending on their meaning, even though they may seem plural in form:

ethics, goods, gross, headquarters, mechanics, politics, series, species, statistics, tactics

Ethics is a subject on which he is well qualified to speak.
His business *ethics are* above question.

Statistics is the only course I failed in school.
The *statistics prove* that I am right.

A *gross* of pencils *is* not enough.
A *gross* of pencils *are* being sent.

These nouns are plural, though they may appear to be singular because they have foreign or unusual plural forms.

> The *analyses* have been completed. (*Analyses* is the plural of *analysis.*)

> What *are* your *bases* for these conclusions? (*Bases* is the plural of *basis.*)

> Some interesting *phenomena are* disclosed in this report. (*Phenomena* is the plural of *phenomenon.*)

> His conclusion seems sound, but his *criteria are* not valid. (*Criteria* is the plural of *criterion.*)

Hyphenated compound nouns usually take their pluralization on the important part.

> editors-in-chief, daughters-in-law

Solid compound nouns always take their pluralization at the end of the word.

> stepdaughters, spoonfuls, bookshelves

Indefinite Pronouns

These indefinite pronouns are singular. When they are used as subjects, they require singular verbs; when used as antecedents, they require singular pronouns.

> anybody, anyone, any one (any one of a group), anything, each, either, every, everybody,

everyone, every one (every one of a group), everything, neither, nobody, no one, nothing, one, somebody, someone, some one (some one of a group), something

Anyone is welcome, as long as *he or she* (not *they*) behaves appropriately.

Any one of the men *is* capable of doing it.

Each of us *is* obliged to sign *his or her* own name.

Either of the alternatives *is* suitable.

Everyone must buy *his or her* book for the course.

Every one of the relatives *wishes* to sign the card.

Everything seems to be going smoothly now.

Neither of the plans *is* workable.

No one believes that our plan will work.

Someone has to finish this dessert.

Even when two indefinite pronouns are joined by *and,* they remain singular in meaning.

Anyone and *everyone is* invited.

Nothing and *no one escapes* her attention.

---

*Written as two words when followed by a phrase.

When *each* or *every* is used to modify a compound subject (subjects joined by *and*), the subject is considered singular.

> *Every ticket holder* and *fan has sent* in a request.

When *each* is inserted (as a parenthetic or explanatory element) between a plural or a compound subject and its plural verb, neither the plural form of the verb nor the plural form of the pronoun is affected.

> Region A, region B, and region C *each expect* to increase *their* investments.

> They *each want* the same thing.

> The customers *each have requested* permission to change *their* method of payment.

Many a (unlike *many*) is singular in meaning and takes a singular verb and pronoun.

> *Many a* new leaf falls prey to insects during its first few weeks.

> But: *Many new leaves* fall prey to insects during *their* first few weeks.

More than one, though its meaning is plural, is used in the singular.

> *More than one* vacation plan *was* changed last night.

> *More than one* detail *is* often overlooked.

These words are plural:

> both, few, many, several, others

> *Both* of us *have received* new assignments.

> *Few will be able* to finish *their* work on time.

> *Many plan* to leave in the morning.

> *Several* writers *have submitted their* stories.

> *Others have* not yet *finished theirs.*

Relative Pronouns

The verb in a relative clause must agree in number and in person with the relative pronoun (*who, which, that, what*) serving as the subject of the clause. The relative pronoun, in turn, must agree with its antecedent. Therefore, before we can make the verb agree with the relative pronoun, we must find the antecedent and determine its person and number.

> Have you talked with the man *who was* waiting to see you? (*Man* is the antecedent of the relative pronoun *who*, and the verb *was* must agree with this antecedent in person and number.)

> Where are the books *that were* left on the table? (The verb in the relative clause—*were*—must agree with the relative pronoun—*that*—which must agree with its antecedent—*books.*)

We *who have* met him do not doubt his ability. (The relative pronoun is *who;* the verb in the relative clause is *have;* the antecedent of the relative pronoun is *we.*)

In sentences that contain the phrases *one of the* or *one of those,* the antecedent of the relative pronoun is not *one,* but the plural words that follow.

One of the tools *that were* on my table has disappeared.

Here is one of the men *who are* moving the piano.

One of the women *who are* attending the conference is wanted on the telephone.

Who, that, or *which* may be used to refer to a collective noun. When the members of the group act, or are considered, as a unit, either *that* or *which* should be used—*that* is usually preferred if the group comprises persons rather than things. *Who* is used when the persons comprising a group act, or are considered, individually.

The editorial suggests that there *is* a *group* of citizens *that* is unhappy with progress.

We have heard from an *association* of homeowners *who feel* strongly opposed to cutting down trees.

Subjects Joined by *and*

When two or more subjects are joined by *and,* whether the subjects are singular or plural, they form a compound subject, which is considered plural.

> The *date and the time* of the party *have* not been decided.

> The *host and his guests are* giving their toasts.

> The *coins, pencils, and other papers are* on the table where you left *them.*

> *He and I* will deliver *our* newspapers in the morning.

Phrases or clauses serving as subjects follow the same rule. When two or more phrases or clauses serving as the subject of a sentence are joined by *and,* the resulting compound subject is considered plural.

> *Rising early in the morning* and *taking a walk before breakfast make* a person feel invigorated all day.

> *That your work is usually done properly* and *that you are usually prompt are* the factors I considered.

EXCEPTION: When the subjects joined by *and* refer to the same person or object or represent a single idea, the whole subject is considered singular.

Ham and eggs is a traditional American breakfast.

The *growth and development* of our country *is* described in this book.

The article or personal pronoun used before each member of the compound subject indicates whether we see the subject as a single idea or as different ideas.

My teacher and friend helps me with my problems. (one person)

My teacher and *my friend help* me with my problems. (two people)

The lead actress and star of the film *has* arrived.

The lead actress and *the star* of the film *have* arrived.

Subjects Joined by *or* or *nor*

When singular subjects are joined by *or* or *nor,* the subject is considered singular.

Neither the *cat nor* the *mouse knows* that *he* is being watched.

One or the *other* of us *has* to go.

Neither *love nor money is* sufficient in such situations.

Neither *heat nor cold nor sun nor wind affects* this material.

When one singular and one plural subject are joined by *or* or *nor,* the subject closer to the verb determines the number of the verb.

I believe that *she or* her *sisters have* the keys to the car.

I believe that her *sisters* or *she has* the keys to the car.

When one antecedent is singular and the other antecedent is plural, the pronoun agrees with the closer antecedent.

Is it the general or the rebels who *merit* praise?

Is it the rebels or the general who *merits* praise?

NOTE: Because your reader may be distracted by your use of a singular verb with a subject containing a plural element, place the plural element nearer the verb whenever possible.

Ask him whether the *card or* the *letters have* been signed.

Neither the *equipment nor* the *drivers are* capable of maintaining that pace.

> When the subjects joined by *or* or *nor* are of different persons, the subject nearer the verb determines its person.
>
> I was told that *she or you were* to be responsible.
>
> I was told that *you or she was* to be responsible.

Shifts in Number or Person

Once you establish a word as either singular or plural, keep it the same throughout the sentence. Be sure that all verbs and all pronouns referring to that word agree with it in number.

Not: Because this *country* bases *its* economy on voluntary compliance with *its* tax laws, we must all pay our share if *they are* to carry out the necessary functions of government.

But: Because this *country* bases *its* economy on voluntary compliance with *its* tax laws, we must all pay our share if *it is* to carry out the necessary function of government.

Not: A *person needs* someone to turn to when *they are* in trouble.

But: A *person needs* someone to turn to when *he or she is* in trouble.

Not: When *one* has had a difficult day, it is important that *they* be able to relax in the evening.

But: When *one* has had a difficult day, it is important that *one* (or *he or she*) be able to relax in the evening.

Be consistent. If you decide that a collective is singular, keep it singular throughout the sentence—use a singular verb to agree with it and a singular pronoun to refer to it. If you establish the collective as plural, see that both the verb and the pronoun are plural.

The committee *has* announced *its* decision.

The committee *have* adjourned and gone to *their* homes.

Our staff *is* always glad to offer *its* advice and assistance.

Most indefinite pronouns are singular and require singular verbs and pronouns.

Not: *Has anyone* turned in *their* report?

But: *Has anyone* turned in *his or her* report?

(The indefinite pronoun *anyone* takes both a singular verb and a singular pronoun.)

Do not apply a verb form from one part of the sentence to another (elliptically) unless the same form is grammatically correct in both parts.

Not: The *numbers were* checked and the total verified.

But: The *numbers were* checked and the *total was* verified.

Avoid shifting the person of pronouns referring to the same antecedent.

Not: When *one* is happy, it often seems as if everyone around *you* is happy, too.

But: When *one* is happy, it often seems as if everyone around *one* (or *him or her*) is happy, too.

Not: *As the ship* entered *her* berth, *its* huge gray shadow seemed to swallow us.

But: As the *ship* entered *its* berth, *its* huge gray shadow seemed to swallow us.

or: As the *ship* entered *her* berth, *her* huge gray shadow seemed to swallow us.

Structure Problems

Usually it is easy for us to identify the subject or antecedent and determine its number and person. But occasionally a puzzling sentence comes along. The subject is there, as clear as can be, but something in the structure of the sentence tries to make us believe that another word is the subject.

Verb Precedes Subject

When the verb precedes the subject in the sentence (either in a question or in a declarative sentence), locate the true subject and make the verb agree with it.

> *Are* the *lamp* and *the bookcase* in this room?

> Walking down the hall *are* the *men* we were waiting for.

> Clearly visible in the sky *were* the *kites* he had previously admired.

> From these books *come some* of our best *ideas*.

> To us *falls* the *task* of repairing the environment.

> Among those attending *were* two former *teachers*.

Where, here, and *there* do not influence the number or person of the verb when introducing a sentence. In such sentences, find the real subject and make the verb agree with it.

> Where *are* the individual *sessions* to be held?
> Where *is* the *case* filed?

> Here *are* the *songs* for which we were waiting.
> Here *is* the *song* for which we were waiting.

There *are* two *books* on the table.
There *is* a *book* on the table.

What, who, which, the interrogative pronouns, do not affect the number of the verb. Again, find the subject of the sentence and make the verb agree with it.

What *is* the *point* of your argument?
What *are* your *recommendations* on this problem?

Who *is* going to accompany you to the dentist?
Who, in this group, *are* members of your family?

Which *is* the *light* that he means?
Which *are* the *standards* that we are to apply?

The expletives *it* or *there* may introduce the verb and stand for the subject, which comes later in the clause. *It* requires a singular verb, even when the real subject is plural. Following *there,* the verb is singular or plural according to the subject which follows it.

It *is solutions* we are looking for, not problems.

It *is* doubtful that he will start today.

There *are* enclosed five copies of the pamphlet you requested.

There *is* attached a letter from your mom.

> **NOTE:** Avoid confusing your reader by using the expletive *it* and the personal pronoun *it* in the same sentence.
>
> Not: I haven't read the book yet; *it* has been hard for me to find time for *it*.
>
> But: I haven't read the *book* yet; I haven't been able to find time for *it*.

Words Intervening between Subject and Verb

The presence of explanatory or parenthetical phrases, or other modifiers, between the subject and verb does not change the number or person of the subject. Locate the real subject of the sentence and make the verb agree with it.

His sworn *statement,* together with statements from other witnesses, *was* heard in court.

The *amount* shown, plus interest, *is* due within 30 days.

The *letter* with its several attachments *was* received this morning.

Our *manners,* like our speech, *are* indicators of character.

The *policeman,* instead of the agents who had been assigned the case, *is* scheduled to visit our neighbor.

His *appraisal,* including extensive notes on the furnishings of the office, *was* well received.

That *fact,* in addition to our already large file on the case, *means* our assumptions were correct.

No one but those present *knows* of this bargain.

Subject and Predicate Differ in Number

After forms of the verb *to be* we often find a construction (called the *predicate nominative*) which means the same thing as the subject. When the predicate nominative differs in number from the subject, the verb must agree with the element that precedes it (the subject).

Our main *problem is* writing complete stories and keeping them short enough for fast reading.

Writing complete stories and keeping them short enough for fast reading are our main problem.

As always, the *question was* sufficient funds.

As always, *sufficient funds were* the question.

The electrician said that a dangerous *problem is* the old lines.

The electrician said that the *old lines are* a dangerous problem.

Construction Shift and Parallelism

Use the same grammatical construction for each of the words or ideas in a sentence if these words or ideas require balance, according to the meaning that the sentence is conveying.

Not: *Singing* and *to dance* are not permitted here.

But: *Singing* and *dancing* (or *To sing* and *to dance*) are not permitted here.

Not: The children are learning the value of *courtesy* and *being kind*.

But: The children are learning the value of *courtesy* and *kindness*.

Special Problems of Pronoun Reference

Pronouns should follow as closely and as logically as possible the antecedent (subject) to which they refer.

Ambiguous Antecedents

Do not use forms of the same pronoun to refer to different antecedents.

Not: The letter is on the conference table *that* we received yesterday.

But: The *letter that* we received yesterday is on the conference table.

Indefinite Antecedents

Be sure that the reference to an antecedent is quite specific.

Not: The copies of these letters were not initialed by the writers, so we are sending *them* back. (What are we sending back? The copies, the letters, or the writers?)

But: We are sending back the copies of the letters because *they* were not initialed by the writers.

Not: When you have finished the book and written your summary, please return *it* to the library. (What is going to be returned, the book or the summary?)

But: When you have finished the book and written your summary, please return the book to the library.

Implied Antecedents

As a general rule, the antecedent of a pronoun must appear in the sentence—not merely be implied. And the antecedent should be a specific word, not an idea expressed in a phrase or clause. *It, which, this,* and *that* are the pronouns that most often lead meaning astray. Any of these pronouns may refer to an idea expressed in a preceding passage if the idea and the reference are *unmistakably* clear. But too often the idea that is unmistakably clear to the speaker or writer is nowhere to be found when the listener or reader looks for it.

Not: Although the doctor operated at once, *it* was not a success and the patient died.

But: Although the doctor performed the *operation* at once, *it* was not a success and the patient died.

or: Although the doctor operated at once, the *operation* was not a success and the patient died.

Vague Reference

The usage illustrated below—the impersonal use of *it, they,* and *you*—is correct, but may produce vague, wordy sentences.

Not: In the instructions *it* says to make three copies.

But: The instructions say to make three copies.

Not: In the letter *it* says he will be here on Thursday.

But: The letter says he will be here on Thursday.

or: He says, in his letter, that he will be here on Thursday.

Not: *They* say in the almanac that we are in for a cold, wet winter.

But: The almanac predicts a cold, wet winter.

Not: From this report *you* can easily recognize the cause of the accident.

But: From this report *one* can easily recognize the cause of the accident. (The first example is correct if the writer is addressing his remarks to a specific person.)

or: The cause of the accident can be easily recognized from this report.

VERBS AND VERBALS

We know that, as their main function, verbs describe an action or a state of being on the part of the subject. But verbs also tell *when* the action took place or *when* the state existed. This property of verbs is called **tense.**

Tense

English has six tenses: three simple tenses (**present, past,** and **future**) in which an action may be considered as simply occurring; and three compound—called **perfect**—tenses in which an action may be considered as completed. (To be *perfected* means to be *completed*.)

Present Tense:	I walk, he walks
Present Perfect Tense:	I have walked, he has walked
Past Tense:	I walked, he walked
Past Perfect Tense:	I had walked, he had walked
Future Tense:	I shall walk, he will walk
Future Perfect Tense:	I shall have walked, he will have walked

Each of the six tenses has a companion form—the **progressive** form. As its name indicates, the progressive says that the action named by the verb is a continued or progressive action. The progressive consists of the present participle (the *-ing* form of the verb—that is, *walking*) plus the proper form of the verb *to be*. The progressive forms of the verb *to walk* are:

Present Tense:	I am walking, he is walking
Present Perfect Tense:	I have been walking, he has been walking
Past Tense:	I was walking, he was walking
Past Perfect Tense:	I had been walking, he had been walking

Future Tense:	I shall be walking, he will be walking
Future Perfect Tense:	I shall have been walking, he will have been walking

The present tense and the past tense also have an **emphatic** form, which uses *do, does, did* as auxiliaries:

Present Tense:	I do understand, she does understand
Past Tense:	You did understand, they did understand

We indicate tense by changing the verb itself or by combining certain forms of the verb with auxiliary verbs. The verb tenses from which we derive every form of a verb are called **principal parts.** The principal parts of a verb are:

The Present Tense:	talk, write
The Past Tense:	talked, wrote
The Present Perfect:	have talked, has written

Verbs are classified as **regular** (or *weak*) and **irregular** (or *strong*), according to the way in which their principal parts are formed. Regular verbs form their past tense and present perfect tense by the addition of *-ed* to the infinitive:

Present Tense	Past Tense	Present Perfect Tense
talk	talked	has (have) talked
help	helped	has (have) helped
walk	walked	has (have) walked

The principal parts of irregular verbs are formed by changes in the verb itself:

Present Tense	Past Tense	Present Perfect Tense
see	saw	has (have) seen
say	said	has (have) said
go	went	has (have) gone

Principal Parts of Troublesome Verbs

Some irregular verbs are particularly troublesome. The following list shows how the principal parts of these irregular verbs change to reflect the tense.

Present Tense	Past Tense	Present Perfect Tense
abide	abode, abided	has abode
arise	arose	has arisen
bear (carry)	bore	has borne
bear (bring forth)	bore	has borne
bid	bade, bid	has bid, bidden
bide	bode, bided	has bode, bided
bleed	bled	has bled
broadcast	broadcast, broadcasted	has broad-cast(ed)
burst	burst	has burst
chide	chid, chidded	has chid, chidded, chidden
choose	chose	has chosen
cleave (adhere)	cleaved	has cleaved
cleave (split)	cleft, cleaved	has cleft, cleaved, cloven
cling	clung	has clung
drink	drank	has drunk

Present Tense	*Past Tense*	*Present Perfect Tense*
drown	drowned	has drowned
flee	fled	has fled
fling	flung	has flung
flow	flowed	has flowed
fly	flew or flied	has flown
forsake	forsook	has forsaken
freeze	froze	has frozen
grind	ground	has ground
hang (a picture)	hung	has hung
hang (a person)	hanged	has hanged
lay (place)	laid	has laid
lead	led	has led
lend	lent	has lent
lie (rest)	lay	has lain
light	lit, lighted	has lit, lighted
raise	raised	has raised
rid	rid, ridded	has rid, ridded
ring	rang	has rung
set	set	has set

Present Tense	Past Tense	Present Perfect Tense
sew	sewed	has sewed, sewn
shrink	shrank, shrunk	has shrunk, shrunken
sink	sank, sunk	has sunk
sit	sat	has sat
ski	skied (rhymes with *seed*)	has skied
slay	slew, slayed	has slain
slide	slid	has slid, slidden
sling	slung	has slung
slink	slunk	has slunk
smite	smote	has smitten
spring	sprang, sprung	has sprung
steal	stole	has stolen
sting	stung	has stung
stink	stank, stunk	has stunk
stride	strode	has stridden
strive	strove, strived	has striven
swim	swam	has swum
swing	swung	has swung

Present Tense	*Past Tense*	*Present Perfect Tense*
thrust	thrust	has thrust
weave	wove, weaved	has woven
wring	wrung	has wrung

NOTE: When two forms are given, one or the other may be restricted to a particular sense of the verb. Consult a dictionary to establish if this is so.

He wove fine cloth.

She weaved in and out of traffic.

Past Tense vs. Past Perfect Tense

The past perfect indicates that the action or condition described was completed (perfected) earlier than some other action that also occurred in the past. Distinguish carefully between this tense and the simple past tense.

When I *came* back from lunch, she *finished* the letter. (Both verbs are in the past tense; therefore, both actions happened at approximately the same time in the past.)

When I *came* back from lunch, she *had finished* the letter. (Again, both actions occurred in the past, but the use of the past perfect *had finished* tells us that this action was completed before the other action.)

We *discovered* that a detective *was following* us. (Both actions happened at the same time in the past.)

We *discovered* that a detective *had been following* us. (He had been following us some time before we discovered it.)

Mood

The mood of a verb tells what kind of utterance is being made. An English verb may be **indicative, imperative,** or **subjunctive** in mood.

Indicative Mood

The indicative mood—used to make a statement or ask a question—is used in almost all our writing and speaking.

The planting *was scheduled* for May 15.

What *is* the correct form to be used?

It *seems* likely to rain.

Imperative Mood

The imperative mood expresses a command, a request, or a suggestion. The subject of an imperative sentence is ordinarily the pronoun *you* (not expressed, simply understood.)

> *Lock* the safe before you leave the office.

> *Let* me give you directions to the interstate.

> Please *sign* the receipt before returning it to us. (Note that the word *please* may be inserted with no effect on the use of the imperative, but often with a desirable effect on the listener or reader.)

Probably the greatest mistake we make in using the imperative mood is in *not using it enough.* An order or a request stated in the imperative is usually not only more emphatic but much more quickly and easily understood.

Indicative:	It would be appreciated if you would open the envelope promptly.
Imperative:	Please open the envelope promptly.

Subjunctive Mood

The subjunctive expresses a hypothetical or conditional situation, or an indirect command. It is going out of use in English, but the subjunctive can still be seen in the following forms:

The third person singular present (which in the indicative has an *-s* and in the subjunctive has none):

Indicative: The plane usually *arrives* on schedule.

Subjunctive: Should the plane *arrive* on schedule, we will be able to make our connection.

Indicative: The detective *prepares* his reports as soon as he completes a case.

Subjunctive: We suggested that the detective *prepare* his reports immediately.

The forms of the verb *be:*

He requested that we *be* there.

If I *were* rich, I would buy a house.

Present: If he *were* able to do it, I am sure he would.

Past: If he *had been* able to do it, I am sure he would have.

Uses of the subjunctive include the following:

1. To express a wish not likely to be fulfilled or impossible to be realized:

    I wish it *were* possible for us to approve the loan. (It is *not* possible.)

    I wish she *were* here to hear your praise of her work. (She is *not* here.)

Would that I *were* able to take this trip in your place. (I am *not* able to go.)

I wish I *were* able to help you.

2. To express a parliamentary motion:

I move that the meeting *be* adjourned.

Resolved, that a committee *be* appointed to study this matter.

3. In a subordinate clause after a verb that expresses a command, a request, or a suggestion:

He asked *that* the flowers *be* watered in his absence.

It is recommended *that* this office *be* responsible for preparing the statements.

We suggest *that* he *be* aware of the situation.

We ask *that* he *consider* the possibility of a reversal.

It is highly desirable *that* they *be* given the keys to the apartment.

4. To express a condition known or supposed to be contrary to fact:

If this *were* up to me, we wouldn't be going.

If I *were* you, I wouldn't wait in the car.

5. After *as if* or *as though*. In formal writing and speech, *as if* and *as though* are followed by the subjunctive, since they introduce as supposition something not factual. In informal writing and speaking, the indicative is sometimes used:

> He talked *as if* he *were* an expert on karate. (He's not.)

> This drawing looks *as though* it *were* the work of a master.

Shifts in Mood

Be consistent in your point of view. Once you have decided on the mood that properly expresses your message, use that mood throughout the sentence or the paragraph. A shift in mood is confusing to the listener or reader; it indicates that the speaker or writer himself has changed his way of looking at the conditions.

Not: The hospital suggests that newborns *be* fed by their mothers and *should be* changed by their fathers. (*Be* is subjunctive; *should be*, indicative.)

But: The hospital suggests that newborns *be* fed by their mothers and *be* changed by their fathers.

Voice

Voice indicates whether the subject of the verb is performing or receiving the action described by the verb. There are two voices: **active** and **passive.**

If the subject is performing the action, the verb is in the active voice.

> The *mechanic fixed* our car.

> The *article summarizes* the problem.

> The *hostess asked* that everyone be seated.

If the subject is being acted upon, the verb is in the passive voice. (The passive form always consists of some form of *be* plus the past participle.)

> Our *car was fixed* by the mechanic.

> The *problem is summarized* in this article.

> *Everyone was asked* by the hostess to be seated.

Active and Passive Voice

In general, the active voice is preferable to the passive: it is simpler and more direct. If, however, you wish to emphasize the action itself or the object of the action and not the agent, use the passive.

> Smoking is prohibited. (emphasizing the object, smoking)

Lori is employed by the college. (emphasizing Lori)

Shifts in Voice

Shifts in voice—often accompanied by shifts in subject—usually occur in compound or complex sentences. Although it is not essential that all clauses in a sentence be the same in structure, any unnecessary shifts may result in a disorganized sentence. Therefore, unless you have a good reason for changing, use the same subject and voice in the second clause that you used in the first.

Not: As *I searched* through my dresser drawers, the missing sock *was found*. (The first subject is *I*—its verb is active; the second subject is *sock*—its verb is passive.)

But: As *I searched* through my dresser drawers, *I found* the missing sock. (Subject is *I* in both clauses; both verbs are active.)

MODIFIERS

Modifiers are words or groups of words that describe, qualify, or limit another word or group of words.

Classification of Modifiers

Modifiers fall generally into two categories: **adjectives** (and phrases or clauses used as adjectives) and

adverbs (and phrases or clauses used as adverbs). Sometimes the form of the modifier clearly shows whether it is an adjective or an adverb; sometimes the form is the same for both.

> Adjectives describe, limit, or make more exact the meaning of a noun or pronoun (any substantive).

> He liked the *red* car.

> The dresser *that is made of oak* is my favorite.

Adverbs describe, limit, or make more exact the meaning of a verb, an adjective, or another adverb.

> He liked the *enchantingly* beautiful actress.

> Run around the track *as quickly as you can*.

Articles

Articles are a type of adjective. The indefinite articles are *a* and *an,* and the definite article is *the.* Use *a* before words beginning with a consonant sound, *an* before those beginning with a vowel sound.

> *a* desk, *a* book

> *an* agent, *an* error, *an* unusual occurrence, *an* honor (the *h* is not pronounced)

The article used before each of two connected nouns or adjectives signals that the words refer to different people or things.

We elected *a* secretary and *a* treasurer. (two persons)

He uses *a* tan and green typewriter. (one machine, two colors)

Do not use *a* or *an* after *sort of, kind of, manner of, style of,* or *type of.*

Not: What *kind of a* book do you want?

But: What *kind of* book do you want?

Do not use *the* before *both.*

Not: We'll buy *the both* of them.

But: We'll buy *both* of them.

The following words may be either adjectives or adverbs depending on their use:

> above, bad, better, cheap, close, deep, early, fast, first, hard, late, long, much, only, quick, slow, very, well

Adverbs with Two Forms

Some adverbs have two forms—one ending in *-ly,* the other not. The longer form is nearly always correct and is preferable in formal writing. The short form is properly used in brief, forceful sentences (in commands, such as the road sign "Drive Slow") and may be used informally. The *-ly* form should, however, always be used to modify an adjective.

Following are examples of adverbs having two forms:

> slow, slowly
> clear, clearly
> quick, quickly

> cheap, cheaply
> sharp, sharply
> loud, loudly

> soft, softly
> deep, deeply
> direct, directly

Sometimes the meaning desired will determine which form should be used. Notice that either *direct* or *directly* may be used when the meaning is "in a straight line," but *directly* is the only choice when *soon* is meant.

NOTE: In informal speech, we sometimes drop the *-ly* ending from some often-used adverbs. This practice is not appropriate in formal writing.

Correct usage:

> I am *really* glad you could come. (Not *real* glad)

Adjectives and Adverbs (Degrees of Comparison)

Adjectives and adverbs change form to show a greater or lesser degree of the characteristic named by the simple word. There are three degrees of comparison.

Positive Degree

The positive degree names the *quality* expressed by the adjective or adverb. It does not imply a comparison with, or a relation to, a similar quality in any other thing.

> *high* morale, a *dependable* worker, work *fast*, prepared *carefully*

Comparative Degree

The comparative degree indicates that the quality described by the modifier exists to a greater or lesser degree in one thing than in another. It is formed by adding *-er* to the positive degree or by inserting *more* or *less* before the positive form.

> Our club has *higher* morale now than ever before.

> Jan is a *more dependable* worker than Tim.

> She can work *faster* than I.

> This meal was prepared *more carefully* than the one we had last night.

Superlative Degree

The superlative degree denotes the greatest or least amount of the quality named. It is formed by adding -*est* to the positive degree of the adjective or adverb or by inserting *most* or *least* before the positive form.

> That club has the *highest* morale of any club.

> Jan is the *most dependable* worker in the office.

> This is the *most carefully* prepared meal I have ever eaten.

The comparative degree is used to refer to only two things, the superlative to more than two.

> This boat is the *longer* of the two.

> This boat is the *longest* of the three.

Using -*er* and -*est* vs. *more* and *most*

There is no difference in meaning between -*er* and *more* or between -*est* and *most*. Either method may be used with some modifiers. However, most adjectives of three syllables or more and almost all adverbs are compared by the use of *more* and *most* (or *less* and *least*) rather than by the endings -*er* and -*est*. In choosing which method should be used with the modifiers that may take either method, you may base your choice on emphasis. By adding -*er* and -*est* to the root word you emphasize the *quality,* while by using *more* or *most* you stress the *degree* of comparison.

Should I have been *kinder* or *harsher* in handling that call?

That boat is the *longest* of the three.

Should I have been *more firm* or *less firm* in handling that caller?

Of all the forms, this one is the *most simple* and that one is the *least simple* to fill out.

Irregular Comparisons

Some modifiers are compared by changes in the words themselves. A few of these irregular comparisons are given below; consult your dictionary whenever you are in doubt about the comparison of any adjective or adverb.

Positive	*Comparative*	*Superlative*
good	better	best
well	better	best
bad (evil, ill)	worse	worst
badly (ill)	worse	worst
far	farther, further	farthest, furthest
late	later, latter	latest, last
little	less, lesser	least
many, much	more	most

Problems with Comparison (Adjectives and Adverbs)

Some adjectives and adverbs express qualities that do not admit freely of comparison. They represent the highest degree of a quality and, as a result, cannot be improved. Some of these words are listed below.

complete	infinitely	square
correct	perfect	squarely
dead	perfectly	supreme
deadly	perpendicularly	totally
exact	preferable	unique
horizontally	round	uniquely
immortally	secondly	universally

However, there may be times when the comparison of these words is justified. If we use these modifiers in a relative or approximate sense, they may be compared. But proceed with care. It is usually better, for example, to say *more nearly round* or *more nearly perfect* than *rounder* or *more perfect*.

Comparison with *other* and *else*

When we use the comparative in such an expression as *this thing is better than any other,* we imply that *this thing* is separate from the group or class to which it is being compared. In these expressions we must use a word such as *other* or *else* to separate the thing being compared from the rest of the group of which it is a part.

Not: Our house is cooler than any house on the block. (The mistake here is not separating the item being compared—*house*—from the group to which it is being compared.)

But: Our house is cooler than any *other* house on the block. (Our house is one of the houses on the block.)

Not: He has a better record than any coach in our conference.

But: He has a better record than any *other* coach in our conference. (He himself is one of the coaches in the conference.)

Incomplete Comparison—Improper Ellipsis
When you make a comparison between two items, be sure that both terms of the comparison are named. Violation of this rule places the burden on the listener or reader, who may or may not clearly understand which of two items you are comparing. Be sure the listener or reader knows exactly what you mean when you say:

There have been more successful ad campaigns in our district this year. (Do you mean *more than in any other district?* or *more than in any previous year?*)

Whenever a comparison is not completed, the meaning of the sentence is obscured.

Incomplete comparison with possessive:

Obscure:	Joe's letter states the problem better than John. (We cannot tell whether it is *John* or *John's letter* that is stating the problem.)
Improved:	Joe's letter states the problem better than *John's.*
Ambiguous:	John's proposed form is less complicated than management.
Improved:	John's proposed form is less complicated than *management's.* (Or: than the one proposed by management.)

Incomplete comparison with conjunction:

Obscure:	This text is as good, if not better than that one. (Because of the omission of the second *as* after *good,* this sentence reads " . . . as good *than.*")

Improved:	This text is as good *as,* if not better than, that one.
or:	This text is as good as that one, if not better.
Obscure:	This book is shorter, but just as comprehensive as that one.
Improved:	This book is shorter *than,* but just as comprehensive as, that one.
or:	This book is shorter than that one, but just as comprehensive.

Incomplete comparison with verb:

Ambiguous:	I enjoy this kind of work more than John. (This could be interpreted as: I enjoy this kind of work more than I enjoy *John.*)
Improved:	I enjoy this kind of work more than John *does.*
Obscure:	I have known him longer than John.
Could mean:	I have known him longer than John *has.*
or:	I have known him longer than *I have known* John.

Split Infinitives

Inserting an adverb between *to* and the rest of an infinitive creates a split infinitive. In the past, writers have been told unequivocally to avoid this construction and to reposition the adverb or recast the entire sentence. Today, however, this rule has been relaxed to a great extent, even by careful writers. Still, avoiding the split infinitive can result in clearer, more graceful writing.

Not: He wished to *completely* forget the matter.

But: He wished to forget the matter *completely.*

Verbals and Verbal Phrases as Modifiers

Verbals are sometimes used as modifiers, either singly or in phrases.

> *To get the most out of the course*, you must study regularly. (infinitive phrase modifying *you*)

> *Rising,* the lion roared. (present participle modifying *lion*)

> The card, *signed by all of us*, was mailed today. (past participles modifying *card*)

> The letter, *having been corrected,* was dropped in the mailbox. (perfect participle modifying *letter*)

Dangling Verbal Phrases

A dangling phrase is one that cannot logically modify the noun or pronoun to which it refers. Corrective action may be taken in either of two ways: (1) by changing the subject of the main clause to one that the phrase can refer to, or (2) by changing the phrase itself into a dependent clause, so that it has a subject of its own.

Dangling:	*To get the most out of this course,* careful *study* is necessary. (The phrase cannot logically modify *study;* it dangles.)
Corrected:	*To get the most out of this course, you* must study it carefully.
or:	If you are to get the most out of this course, you must study it carefully.
Dangling:	*To apply for this job*, an *application* must be completed. (Dangles; an *application* can't apply.)
Corrected:	*To apply for this job,* the *applicant* must complete an applicaton.
or:	When the applicant applies for the job, an application must be completed.

Dangling: *By summarizing the information,* a clear *picture* of the situation was presented. (Dangles; a picture cannot perform the act of summarizing information.)

Corrected: *By summarizing the information, we* were able to present a clear picture of the situation.

or: After we had summarized the information, a clear picture of the situation was presented.

An infinitive or a participial phrase that modifies the whole sentence—designating general action rather than action by a specific agent—may be correctly used without relation to the subject of the main clause.

> *Generally speaking,* these plants grow better in sunlight.

> *To summarize,* Albuquerque has many spectacular sunsets.

Prepositional Phrases as Modifiers

The prepositional phrase can serve as an adjective or adverb.

> The letter was addressed to the office *of the registrar.* (adjective modifying *office*)

They have gone *to the rally.* (adverb modifying *have gone*)

A prepositional phrase *dangles* when it does not, both logically and grammatically, refer to the subject of the main clause.

Dangling: *With much effort,* the *assignment* was completed on time.

Corrected: *With much effort, we* completed the assignment on time.

Dependent Clauses as Modifiers

Dependent clauses can serve as adjectives or adverbs. Parts of a dependent clause are sometimes omitted because the missing elements can be easily supplied. These incomplete clauses are known as **elliptical clauses.** An elliptical clause must be able to modify, both logically and grammatically, the subject of the main clause. If it does not, it dangles.

Dangling: *Unless compiled by early June,* we cannot include the figures in this year's crop report.

Corrected: *Unless compiled by early June,* the figures cannot be included in this year's crop report.

or: Unless *the figures are* compiled by early June, we cannot include them in this year's crop report.

Dangling: *While making his periodic tour of the state,* a few changes in the planned itinerary were necessary.

Corrected: *While making his periodic tour of the state,* he made a few changes in the planned itinerary.

or: While *he was* making his periodic tour of the state, a few changes in planned itinerary were made.

Relative Pronouns Introducing Clauses

Be careful to select the correct relative pronoun to introduce the adjective clause. *Who* refers to persons; *what, that,* and *which* refer to things; *that* usually refers to things, but is sometimes used to refer to persons.

The trainer *who tamed this lion* has had extensive experience.

The homework assignment, *which is due tomorrow,* will contain that information.

The time card *that you have been submitting weekly* will be required once a month from now on.

Placement of Modifiers

Modifiers should be placed as close as possible to the words they modify. This is true whether the modifier is a single word, a phrase, or a clause. In English, sometimes the only way the reader can tell which word is being modified is by the location of the modifier. It's often simply a matter of proximity.

Many ambiguous (and unintentionally humorous) sentences result from the misplacement of modifiers.

Modifier between Subject and Verb

Wherever possible, avoid placing the modifier between subject and verb and between verb and object.

Not: The driver, *to save money on fuel,* switched to a smaller car.

But: *To save money on fuel,* the driver switched to a smaller car.

Single Adverbs

Some adverbs—*only, almost, nearly, also, quite, merely, actually*—are frequent troublemakers. Be sure they are placed as close as possible to the words they modify.

Example: The problem can *only* be defined by this committee.

Could mean:	*Only* this committee can define the problem.
or:	This committee can *only define* the problem, not solve it.

Do not use *hardly, only, scarcely, barely*—so-called subtractive adverbs—together with a negative construction. If you do, you will have a double negative.

Not:	They *haven't only* a single blanket.
But:	They *have only* a single blanket.
Not:	He *hasn't scarcely* done anything worthwhile.
But:	He *has scarcely* done anything worthwhile.

Phrases and Clauses
Phrases and clauses, like single-word modifiers, should be placed as close as possible to the words they modify; this way there will be no danger of their attaching themselves to the wrong sentence element.

Not:	We need someone to design buildings *with architectural experience.*
But:	We need someone *with architectural experience* to design buildings.
Not:	Mr. Dough has resigned from Congress after having served four years *to the regret of all the members.*

But: *To the regret of all the members,* Mr. Dough has resigned from Congress after having served four years.

Relative Clauses

Relative clauses should also be placed immediately after the word they modify, since they attach themselves to the sentence element nearest them.

Not: The man has an appointment *who is waiting in my office.*

But: The man *who is waiting in my office* has an appointment.

Not: She mentioned the number of cases closed by agents in her group *which are over a year old.*

But: She mentioned the number of cases *over a year old* which have been closed by agents in her group.

Squinting Constructions

Avoid **squinting** constructions—that is, modifiers that are so placed that one cannot tell whether they are modifying the words immediately preceding them or those immediately following them.

Obscure: The city agreed *after the papers were signed* to allow the march.

Could mean:	The city agreed to allow the march *after the papers were signed.*
or:	*After the papers were signed,* the city agreed to allow the march.

Obscure:	He agreed *that morning* to marry her.
Could mean:	He agreed to marry her *that morning*.
or:	*That morning,* he agreed to marry her.

CONNECTIVES

Four kinds of words can serve as connectives: **prepositions, conjunctions, relative pronouns,** and **relative adverbs.** Each not only connects two sentence elements but also shows the relationship between them.

Prepositions

A preposition *connects* the word, phrase, or clause that follows it (its object) with some other element in the sentence *and shows the relationship* between them. A preposition can be a single word (*to, with*) or a phrase (*according to, as well as, because of, contrary to*).

Prepositional Idioms

The use of many prepositions in English is purely idiomatic: there is no logical reason that one preposition is wrong and another correct in a given expression. There are no rules for choosing the correct preposition; the idioms must simply be memorized. Study the following list of some of the more common prepositional idioms.

accede **to**	We cannot *accede to* the request.
accessory **of**	He was an *accessory of* the criminal.
accessory **to**	He was an *accessory to* the act.
accommodate **to**	He finds it hard to *accommodate* himself *to* new situations. (changed conditions)
accommodate **with**	We *accommodated* her *with* a loan of five dollars.
accompany **by**	Sheba was *accompanied by* a friend. (a person)
accompany **with**	The flowers were *accompanied with* a note. (a thing)
accountable **for**	I am *accountable for* my actions.
accountable **to**	I am *accountable to* my parents.

accused **by**	He was *accused by* the customer of giving poor service.
accused **of**	Edwin was *accused of* eating the last cookie.
acquiesce **in**	The commissioner *acquiesced in* the decision.
acquit **of**	The group was *acquitted of* the crime.
acquit **with**	She *acquitted* herself *with* honor.
adapt **for**	The stairway was *adapted for* our use.
adapt **from**	The movie was *adapted from* the book.
adapt **to**	Evelyn finds it difficult to *adapt to* new procedures.
adequate **for**	His golf game was not *adequate for* the course.
adequate **to**	Her ability was *adequate to* the job.
averse **to**	Fernandez was not *averse to* hard work.

advise **of**	The skaters were *advised of* the new regulations.
affix **to**	A stamp was *affixed to* the container.
agree **on**	They cannot *agree on* the best course of action.
agree **to**	They state that they *agree to* the compromise.
agree **with**	The boys and their fathers *agree with* us.
amenable **to**	Francis was *amenable to* our suggestion.
analogous **to**	This situation is *analogous to* the one we faced last year.
annoy **by**	The librarian was *annoyed by* the frequent interruptions.
annoy **with**	I was *annoyed with* many of the suggestions.
apparent **in**	Marv's attitude is *apparent in* his actions.
apparent **to**	The trouble is *apparent to* everyone.

append **to**	A rider was *appended to* the bill.
appreciation **for**	The student had a deep *appreciation for* the arts.
appreciation **of**	He expressed *appreciation of* their hard work.
appreciative **of**	They are *appreciative of* Jim's efforts.
authority **in**	Dr. Rollin is an *authority in* the field of radiology.
authority **on**	Professor Haslem is an *authority on* Renaissance literature.
basis **for**	They had a sound *basis for* agreement.
basis **in**	Janet's argument has no *basis in* fact.
cater **to**	This magazine *caters to* coin collectors.
commensurate **with**	His salary was *commensurate with* his abilities.
comply **with**	We must *comply with* the request.

concur **in**	We *concur in* the decision of the survey committee.
concur **with**	One member did not *concur with* the others.
conform **to**	All campers must *conform to* the regulations.
consist **in**	Her chief value *consists in* her ability to work with others.
consist **of**	The handbook *consists of* mathematical formulas.
consistent **in**	Parents should be *consistent in* rearing their children.
correspond **to**	His description of the planet *corresponds to* the known facts.
correspond **with**	Lakeisha has been *corresponding with* her boyfriend.
demand **from**	What did Oscar *demand from* them in payment?
demand **of**	They had *demanded* an accounting *of* the company funds.

differ **from**	Trent's estimate of the amount due *differs from* Jarlyn's.
differ **in**	We *differ in* our political opinions.
differ **on**	They *differ on* the amount to be assessed.
differ **with**	I *differ with* him about the evaluation method to be used.
discrepancy **between**	There is a *discrepancy between* the two totals.
discrepancy **in**	There is a *discrepancy in* Felix's account.
displeased **at**	Jeff was *displeased at* the way the employee wasted time.
displeased **with**	Rolando was *displeased with* Michael's comments.
eligible **for**	He is *eligible for* the job.
equivalent **in**	His shirt and mine are *equivalent in* size.
equivalent **of**	This is the *equivalent of* a full payment.

equivalent **to**	Each payment is *equivalent to* a week's salary.
excepted **from**	He was *excepted from* further responsibility.
excluded **from**	This item may be *excluded from* the questionnaire.
exempt **from**	This type of income is *exempt from* tax.
expect **from**	What favor do you *expect from* your friend?
expect **of**	What does Bacon *expect of* his assistant?
familiar **to**	The name is *familiar to* me.
familiar **with**	I am quite *familiar with* motorcycles.
find **for**	The jury *found for* the defendant.
furnish **to**	Adequate supplies were *furnished to* them.
furnish **with**	Please *furnish* us *with* background information on this matter.
habit **of**	Carlos made a *habit of* checking his facts.

identical **with**	That case is *identical with* the one I am working on.
identify **by**	The girl was *identified by* the tattoo on her arm.
identify **with**	He was *identified with* the opposing members.
ignorant **of**	He was *ignorant of* his rights.
improvement **in**	The *improvement in* his singing was soon noted.
improvement **on**	His second pasta dish was an *improvement on* the first.
inconsistent **with**	Cruelty is *inconsistent with* civilized behavior.
infer **from**	We *infer from* Karen's statement that she plans to visit Paul.
influence **by**	The actors were all *influenced by* the director's exhortations.
influence **on (upon)**	The moon at perigee has a dramatic *influence on (upon)* the tides.

influence **over**	The minister had a strong *influence over* his congregation.
influence **with**	Mark referred frequently to his *influence with* those in authority.
inform **of**	Patients should keep their doctors *informed of* any changes in their health.
inherent **in**	A capacity for growth is *inherent in* all people.
insert **in**	This pin should be *inserted in* the slot.
intercede **for**	My best friend *interceded for* me.
intercede **with**	Doug *interceded with* the board in my behalf.
invest **in**	The police said he had *invested* the money *in* stocks.
invest **with**	She was *invested with* full power to act.
irrelevant **to**	This statement is *irrelevant to* the matter under discussion.

irrespective **of**	They decided to appoint him *irrespective of* the criticism that might result.
liable **for**	Trudi is *liable for* damages.
liable **to**	The employee is *liable to* his employer.
liberal **in**	He was very *liberal in* his views.
liberal **with**	My boss was *liberal with* her praise.
necessity **for**	There is no *necessity for* our launching the boat.
necessity **of**	We are faced with the *necessity of* reducing travel expenses.
oblivious **of (to)**	He was *oblivious of (to)* the effect that his remarks had on his friends.
precedent **for**	Is there a *precedent for* this action?
precedent **in**	His decision established a *precedent in* law.

recompense **for**	Miguel was fully *recompensed for* the time he spent on the job.
reconcile **to**	We have become *reconciled to* our fate.
reconcile **with**	Our views cannot be *reconciled with* his.
similarity **in**	I agree that there is much *similarity in* their appearance.
similarity **of**	The *similarity of* these odd vegetables caused a great deal of confusion.
similarity **to**	This camera shows a *similarity to* one I have.
talk **of**	The traveler *talked* long *of* his experiences.
talk **to**	The teacher *talked to* his class.
talk **with**	The lawyer *talked with* her client.
transfer **from**	He has been *transferred from* his former position.

transfer **to**	They *transferred* him *to* another department.
unequal **in**	The contestants were *unequal in* strength.
unequal **to**	She was *unequal to* the demands placed on her.
use **for**	He had no *use for* the extra table.
use **of**	She made good *use of* her opportunity.
wait **for**	Marci seemed to be *waiting for* someone.

Placement of Prepositions

It is now considered acceptable to end a sentence with a preposition.

> What did you do that *for?*

> We had too many ideas to talk *about.*

Superfluous Prepositions

In formal writing, avoid superfluous prepositions.

Not: He is standing near *to* the ledge.

But: He is standing near the ledge.

Not: When are you going to start *in* to write that
        letter?

But: When are you going to start to write that
        letter?

Faulty Omission of Prepositions

The preference in more formal writing is to repeat
the preposition before the second of two connected
elements.

> He seemed interested *in* us and our problems.
> He seemed interested *in* us and *in* our problems.

> He was able to complete the renovation *by* plan-
> ning carefully and working diligently.
> He was able to complete the renovation *by* plan-
> ning carefully and *by* working diligently.

In the so-called *split* (or *suspended*) construction, in
which two words are completed by different prepositions, be especially careful to use both prepositions.

Not: He has an interest and an aptitude *for* his
        work.

But: He has an interest *in* and an aptitude *for*
        his work. (Commas may be used in this
        construction: He has an interest in, and an
        aptitude for, his work.)

Not: They were puzzled and concerned *about*
        her erratic behavior.

But: They were puzzled *by* and concerned *about* her erratic behavior.

Conjunctions and Parallelism

Sentence elements are said to be *coordinate* (or *parallel*) when they are of equal rank (of equal importance) both grammatically and logically.

Determining equal grammatical importance is relatively simple: words = words; phrases = phrases; subordinate clauses = subordinate clauses; principal clauses = principal clauses.

Elements not grammatically equal (not parallel) are shown in this example:

> His main virtues are *that he is sincere* and *his generosity*. (a clause linked to a word)

Improved:

> His main virtues are *that he is sincere* and *that he is generous*. (two noun clauses, now parallel; noun clause = noun clause)

> His main virtues are his *sincerity* and his *generosity*. (two words)

Coordinate Conjunctions Showing Coordination (Parallelism)

The coordinate conjunctions, including *and, but, or, nor, for, yet, moreover,* are the connectives most frequently used to show that two ideas are equal (are parallel). Notice in the following illustrations that the two ideas connected are parallel.

> The *director and* the *assistant director* will attend the meeting. (connecting a word with a word)

> He is a man *of great capability but of little experience.* (connecting a phrase with a phrase)

> He said *that he had filed a claim for a refund but that he had not heard anything further from this store.* (connecting a subordinate clause with a subordinate clause)

> *I was eager to attend the seminar; moreover, I knew that the exchange of ideas would be helpful.* (connecting an independent clause with an independent clause)

Correlative Conjunctions Showing Coordination (Parallelism)

The correlative conjunctions—*either . . . or, neither . . . nor, not only . . . but also, both . . . and, if . . . then, since . . . therefore*—work in pairs to show that words and ideas are parallel (equal in importance).

> *Either* the *doctor or* the *lawyer* must attend. (connecting a word with a word)

> The report is designed *not only to present a list of the problems facing us but also* to *recommend*

possible solutions to these problems. (connecting a phrase with a phrase)

The significant point in the use of pairs of correlatives is that each member of the pair must be followed by the same part of speech (same grammatical construction). That is, if *not only* is followed by a verb, then *but also* must be followed by a verb; if *either* is followed by a phrase, *or* must likewise be followed by a phrase.

Not: *Either* fish of this type are much fewer in number *or* are not easily caught. (*Either* is followed by a noun, *fish;* or is followed by a verb phrase.)

But: Fish of this type *either* are much fewer in number *or* are not easily caught.

Not: His reply *not only* was prompt *but also* complete.

But: His reply was *not only* prompt *but also* complete.

When this plan is not followed, the result is "faulty parallelism." To turn faulty parallelism into effective parallelism, sometimes we need add only a word or two.

Not: The picnic was a disappointment *not only* to me *but also* my boyfriend. (*Not only* is

followed by the prepositional phrase *to me;
but also* is followed by a noun.)

But: The picnic was a disappointment *not only*
to me *but also* to my boyfriend. (Note that
each of the correlative conjunctions is followed by a prepositional phrase.)

Not: His assignment was *both* to conduct the
course *and* the evaluation of it.

But: His assignment was *both* to conduct the
course *and* to evaluate it.

NOTE: The correlative *as . . . as* is used both
affirmatively and negatively; the correlative *so . . .
as* is used only negatively.

This melon is *as* sweet *as* that one.

This melon is not *as* sweet *as* that one

This melon is not *so* sweet *as* that one.

Troublesome Conjunctions

and *vs.* also

Also, a weak connective, should not be used in place
of *and* in sentences such as:

He writes poems, stories, *and* (not *also*) art re-
views.

and etc.

The abbreviation *etc.* stands for the Latin *et cetera,* meaning *and so forth.* Obviously, then, an additional *and* is not only unnecessary but incorrect.

Not: He used all our paper, pencils, pens, *and etc.*

But: He used all our paper, pencils, pens, *etc.*

and which, and who, but which

Avoid using *and which, and who, but which, but that,* etc., when there is no preceding *who, which,* or *that* in the sentence to complete the parallel construction.

Not: We are looking for a car more economical to operate *and which* will be easy to maintain.

But: We are looking for a car *which* will be more economical to operate *and which* will be easy to maintain.

***too many* and's**

Avoid stringing together a group of sentence elements connected by *and's.*

Not: The evaluation of the training program was planned *and* conducted *and* reported to the appropriate officials.

But: The evaluation of the training program was planned *and* conducted; then it was reported to the appropriate officials.

and *vs.* but
Use *and* to show addition; use *but* to show contrast.

Not: The boy and his mother have been called
         to a short meeting, *and* the principal will be
         out of the office all afternoon.

But: The boy and his mother have been called
         to a short meeting, *but* the principal will be
         out of the office all afternoon.

and *or* but *to begin a sentence*
We may begin a sentence—or even a paragraph—
with *and, but,* or any other coordinating conjunction. A coordinate conjunction or a conjunctive adverb at the beginning of a sentence is often a handy
signpost for the reader, pointing out the direction this
new sentence will carry him.

as, since, because
These conjunctions can be used interchangeably to
introduce clauses of cause or reason.

> *Because* the book was due at the library, I re-
> turned it.

> *Since* the book was due at the library, I re-
> turned it.

> *As* the book was due at the library, I returned it.

However, *since* and *as* have another function: *since*
introduces clauses of sequence of time, and *as*

introduces clauses of duration of time. Because of the double function of these two words, we must be careful to use them only in sentences in which they cannot be misunderstood.

Not: *Since* this study was conducted to analyze the effects of . . . (Could mean: *Since the time that* the study was conducted . . .)

But: *Because* this study was conducted to analyze the effects of . . .

Not: *As* I was writing the lab report, he gave the correct answers to Beth. (Could mean: *During the time that* I was writing the lab report . . .)

But: *Because* I was writing the lab report . . .

NOTE: When an *as* or *since* clause comes last in the sentence, the meaning of the conjunction can be made clear by the punctuation of the clause. If *as* or *since* is used as a time indicator, the clause it introduces is not set off from the sentence. But if the conjunction introduces a clause of cause or reason, the clause is set off.

There have been several changes in policy *since* the committee released its findings. (No punctuation; *since* means *since the time that.*)

There have been several changes in policy, *since* the committee released its findings. (... *because* the committee released its findings)

as vs. that or whether
Avoid using *as* in place of *that* or *whether* to introduce clauses following such verbs as *say, think, know*.

Not: I don't know *as* I believe you.

But: I don't know *that* I believe you.

or: I don't know *whether* I believe you.

if *vs.* whether
If is used to introduce clauses of condition or supposition.

> We will stay *if* the fish are biting.

> *If* you cannot answer the phone immediately, please ask Erin to do it.

Whether introduces clauses indicating an alternative. The alternative may be expressed in the sentence or understood.

> It will not make any difference *whether* John agrees or disagrees with the outcome of the polling.

Please let me know *whether* you received the check.

Today, many grammarians endorse the use of either *if* or *whether* in such constructions as

Please let me know *if* (or *whether*) you received the check.

I wonder *if* (or *whether*) he is qualified for that position.

If there is any danger that the reader may fail to understand the meaning, use the preferred *whether*.

whether *vs.* whether or not
It is not essential that *or not* be used with *whether* to complete the alternative choice. These words may be added if they are needed for emphasis.

Either: Please let me know *whether or not* you received our letter.

Or: Please let me know *whether* you received our letter.

that *introducing parallel clauses*
When either *that* or *which* introduces one of a series of parallel clauses, the same conjunction must introduce the other clauses in the series. Do not shift conjunctions or omit the conjunction in later clauses.

Not: He said *that* he would call me before noon
        and his brother would meet me. (conjunc-
        tion omitted)

But: He said *that* he would call me before
        noon and *that* his brother would meet me.
        (conjunction supplied)

Shift in conjunction:

Not: We painted the boat *that* we liked so much
        and *which* we bought.

But: We painted the boat *that* we liked so much
        and *that* we bought.

proper omission of that

That may be omitted in noun clauses (especially those
following such verbs as *say, think, feel, believe, hope*)
and in adjective clauses, if the meaning of the sentence is clear.

Noun clauses:

   He said (*that*) he would call me before noon.

   I hope (*that*) we can finish this painting today.

Adjective clauses:

   The book (*that*) I asked for is out on loan.

   The instructions (*that*) she gave were perfectly
   clear.

faulty repetition of that

Do not use *that* twice to introduce the same noun clause. This error most often occurs in a long sentence in which a long interrupting expression occurs between *that* and the rest of its clause.

Not: I am sure you can appreciate *that,* in order to serve as many guests as possible, *that* we must open the veranda.

But: I am sure you can appreciate *that,* in order to serve as many guests as possible, we must open the veranda.

when

Avoid using *when* to introduce a definition unless the definition pertains to time.

Not: Their first important step in the improvement of the conditions was *when* they thoroughly surveyed the situation. (The step was not "when.")

But: Their first important step in the improvement of the conditions was *the thorough survey* of the situation.

Correct usage: Three o'clock is *when* the meeting will be held.

where

Avoid using *where* to introduce a definition unless the definition pertains to place or location.

Not: A sentence is *where* you have a subject and a verb. (A sentence is not "where.")

But: A sentence is a group of words containing a subject and a verb.

Correct The large conference room is *where* the
usage: meeting is being held.

Avoid substituting *where* for *that*.

Not: I saw in the bulletin *where* the new law has been put into effect.

But: I saw in the bulletin *that* the new law has been put into effect.

while *vs.* when

While indicates duration of time; *when* indicates a fixed or stated period of time.

When I return to work, I will take you out to lunch. (at that fixed time)

While I am shopping, I will look for that skirt. (During the time I am shopping . . .)

while *vs.* though, although, and, but

While pertains to time and should not be substituted loosely for though, although, whereas, and, or but.

Not: *While* I did not remember the woman's name, I thought I could recognize her face.

But: *Although* I did not remember the woman's name, I thought I could recognize her face.

Not: I assembled the material for the manual *while* he wrote the outline. (Could mean: *during the time that he . . .*)

But: I assembled the material for the manual, *but* he wrote the outline.

PUNCTUATION

The purpose of punctuation is to clarify the meaning of written language. In general, punctuation marks should prevent misreading by bringing out clearly the author's intended meaning.

APOSTROPHE

Do not space to set off an apostrophe.

1. In a contraction, insert an apostrophe in place of the omitted letter or letters.

    have + not = haven't

    we + are = we're

    let + us = let's

    class of 2001 = class of '01

2. When indicating possession, the apostrophe means *belonging to everything to the left of the apostrophe.*

    lady's = belonging to the lady

ladies' = belonging to the ladies

children's = belonging to the children

Observe the following forms:

man's, men's

hostess's, hostesses'

prince's, princes'

In set phrases, nouns ending in *-s* or *-ce* and followed by a word beginning with an *s* may form the possessive by adding an apostrophe only, with no following *s*.

for goodness' sake   for old times' sake

In compound nouns, the *'s* is added to the element nearest the object possessed.

comptroller general's office

John White, Jr.'s account

attorney at law's fee

Joint possession is indicated by placing an apostrophe on the last element of a series; individual or alternative possession requires the use of an apostrophe on each element in the series.

soldiers and sailors' home

Brown & Nelson's store

men's, women's, or children's clothing

editor's or proofreader's opinion

Possessive pronouns do not take an apostrophe.

its (belongs to it)   theirs

Do not confuse *its* with the contraction *it's* (it is).

3. Use an apostrophe to form the plural of numbers and letters, and words referred to as words.

49'ers	a's, 7's, ¶'s
YMCA's	three R's
2's, 3's,	*but* twos and threes

Observe the following forms:

ands, ifs, and buts   ins and outs

do's and don'ts

Years may be typed as follows:

1990's or 1990s, the '90s, *not* the '90's

BRACKETS

Do not space to set off brackets from the material they enclose.

1. Brackets are used to enclose interpolations that are not specifically a part of transcribed or quoted material. An interpolation in brackets is often a correction, an explanation, or a warning that the material quoted is in error.

   "The bill had *not* been paid." [Emphasis added.]

   "July 3 [sic] is a national holiday."

2. Brackets are used to enclose parenthetical material within a parenthesis.

   (The result [see fig. 2] is most surprising.)

COLON

Check carefully the spacing for colons. See each example below.

1. Use a colon after the salutation in a business letter.

   Dear Board Member:

2. Use a colon (or a slash) to separate the initials of the dictator from the initials of the typist. Do not space after the colon.

   RLT:pop

3. Use a colon to separate hours from minutes. Do not space after the colon.

   The eclipse occurred at 10:36 A.M.

4. A colon may (but need not always) be used to introduce a list, a long quotation, and a question.

   My question is this: Are you willing to punch a time clock?

5. Use a colon before a final clause that extends or explains what is said in the preceding matter.

   Railroading is not a variety of outdoor sport: it is a service.

6. Use a colon to indicate proportion and a double colon to indicate ratio. Space before and after the colon.

   concrete mixed 5 : 3 : 1

   1 : 2 :: 4 : 12

COMMA

Leave one space after the comma.

1. The salutation of a personal letter is followed by a comma.

   Dear Mary,

2. The complimentary close of a letter is ordinarily followed by a comma, though this use is optional.

> Cordially yours,

3. An appositive must be set off by commas.

> Jim Rodgers, my next-door neighbor, is an excellent baby-sitter.

4. A noun of address is set apart by commas.

> When you finish your homework, Jeff, please take out the garbage.

5. Use commas to set off parenthetical words.

> I think, however, that move might not be wise at this time.

6. When two or more adjectives (called coordinate adjectives) all modify a noun equally, all but the last must be followed by commas. Test: if you can add the word *and* between the adjectives without changing the sense of the sentence, then use commas.

> The jolly, fat man stood at the top of the stairs.

7. An introductory phrase or clause of five or more words is usually followed by a comma.

> Because the prisoner had a history of attempted jailbreaks, he was put under heavy guard.

8. After a short introductory phrase, the comma is optional. The comma should be used where needed for clarity.

> As a child she was a tomboy. (comma unnecessary)

> To Dan, Phil was friend as well as brother. (comma clarifies)

> In 1978, 300 people lost their lives in one air disaster. (comma clarifies)

9. A comma is not generally used before a subordinate clause that ends a sentence, though in long, unwieldy sentences, use of such a comma is optional.

10. A comma precedes the coordinating conjunction unless the two clauses are very short.

> The boy wanted to borrow a book from the library, but the librarian would not allow him to take it until he had paid his fines.

> Roy washed the dishes and Helen dried them.

11. Words, phrases, or clauses in a series are separated by commas. The use of a comma before

and is optional. If the series ends in *etc.*, use a comma before *etc.* Do not use a comma after *etc.* in a series, even if the sentence continues.

> Coats, umbrellas, and boots should be placed in the closet at the end of the hall.

> Pencils, scissors, paper clips, etc. belong in your top desk drawer.

12. A comma separates a short direct quotation from the speaker.

> She said, "I must leave work on time today."

> "Tomorrow I begin my new job," he told us.

13. Use a comma to indicate that you have omitted a word or words, such as *of* or *of the*.

> President, XYZ Corporation

14. Use a comma to separate a name from a title or personal-name suffix.

> Linda Feiner, Chairman

> Carl Andrew Pforzheimer, Jr.

15. Use a comma when first and last names are reversed.

> Bernbach, Melissa

16. Use a comma to separate parts of addresses.

> Please come to a party at "The Old Mill" on Drake Road, Cheswold, Delaware.

The use of a comma between the name of a city and a two-letter postal abbreviation of a state is optional. Do not use a comma between the postal abbreviation of a state and the zip code.

> Cleveland OH 44114   Scarsdale, NY 10583

17. A comma may or may not be used to separate parts of a date. But note that in European and military style dates the comma is never used.

> We will be leaving for Paris on October 6, 1999.

> I think she will arrive on April 14 1998.

> He joined the navy 31 October 1956.

18. A comma ordinarily separates thousands, millions, billions, and trillions. There is no space before or after the comma.

> 75,281,646

19. A nonrestrictive adjective phrase or clause must be set off by commas. A nonrestrictive phrase or clause is one that can be omitted without changing the meaning of the sentence.

Our new sailboat, which has bright orange sails, is very seaworthy.

A restrictive phrase or clause is vital to the meaning of a sentence and cannot be omitted. Do not set it off with commas.

A sailboat without sails is useless.

20. A comma must be used if the sentence might be subject to different interpretation without it.

He saw the woman who had rejected him, and blushed.

21. If a pause would make the sentence clearer and easier to read, insert a comma.

Inside the people were dancing. (confusing)

Inside, the people were dancing. (clearer)

After all crime must be punished. (confusing)
After all, crime must be punished. (clearer)

The pause rule is not infallible, but it is an acceptable resort when all other comma rules fail to suit the situation.

DASH

Leave no space on either side of a dash.

1. You may use a dash—or parentheses—for emphasis or to set off an explanatory group of words.

   > The tools of his trade—probe, mirror, cotton swabs—were neatly arranged on the dentist's tray.

2. Dashes must be used in pairs unless the set-off expression ends a sentence or marks a sudden break in thought or speech that leaves a sentence unfinished.

   > The elections will take place in November— if we remain at peace.

   > "No! Don't open that—"

ELLIPSIS

An ellipsis is three spaced periods. If the material deleted includes a final period, type four spaced periods.

1. An ellipsis indicates that something has been left out of a quoted text.

"The country is excited from one end to the
other by a great question of principle. On that
question the Government has taken one side."

becomes

"The country is excited . . . by a great question . . . . On that question the Government
has taken one side."

2. Four spaced periods may be used to indicate that
a sentence or more has been omitted. To indicate the omission of an entire paragraph or more,
terminate the preceding paragraph with a period and ellipsis (four dots) and initiate the next
paragraph with an ellipsis (three dots).

EXCLAMATION MARK

Leave two spaces after the exclamation mark.

1. An exclamation mark indicates strong feeling
or emotion.

Congratulations! You broke the record.

Rush! Perishable contents.

Don't touch that dial!

HYPHEN

There is no space on either side of a hyphen unless it is used at the end of the line.

1. Use a hyphen to divide a word at the end of a line.

2. Use a hyphen to connect the elements of some compounds. (See the section on Compound Words.)

3. Use a hyphen to separate the letters of a spelled word.

> In front of the children she asked me if I had brought the c-a-n-d-y.

PARENTHESES

Do not space to set off parentheses from the material they enclose.

1. Use parentheses to set off matter that is not intended to be part of the main statement or that is not a grammatical element of the sentence, yet important enough to be included.

> This case (124 US 329) is not relevant.

> The result (see fig. 2) is most surprising.

> The Galesburg (IL) Chamber of Commerce

A reference in parentheses at the end of a sentence is placed before the period, unless it is a complete sentence in itself.

The specimens show great variation. (See pl. 6.)

The specimens show great variation (pl. 6).

2. Use parentheses to enclose a figure following a spelled-out number in a legal document.

The tenant shall vacate within thirty (30) days.

3. Use parentheses to enclose numbers or letters designating items in a series.

The order of delivery will be (a) food, (b) medicines, and (c) clothing.

PERIOD

Leave two spaces after the period at the end of a sentence.

1. Use a period at the end of a sentence that makes a statement, gives a command, or makes a polite request in the form of a question that does not require an answer.

I am brushing up on my archery skills.

Give generously of yourself.

Please read that menu to me.

2. Use a period after some abbreviations, including the initials of a personal name. (See the comprehensive section in this volume on abbreviations.)

   Gen. Robert E. Lee led the Confederate forces.

3. Use a period as a decimal point in numbers. Do not leave a space before or after the period.

   A sales tax of 5.5 percent amounts to $7.47 on a $135.80 purchase.

QUESTION MARK

Leave two spaces after the question mark.

1. Use a question mark at the end of a direct and genuine question.

   Why do you wish to return to Peru?

2. Do not use a question mark after an indirect question; use a period.

   He asked if they wanted to accompany him.

   I wonder where the fire is.

3. A direct question must end with a question mark even if the question does not encompass the entire sentence.

"Daddy, are we there yet?" the child asked.

The man cried "Who would do such a thing?" when he saw his vandalized car.

4. Use a question mark (within parentheses) to indicate uncertainty as to the correctness of a fact.

John Carver, first governor of Plymouth colony, was born in 1575 (?) and died in 1621.

QUOTATION MARKS

Do not space to set off quotation marks from the material they enclose.

1. All directly quoted material must be enclosed by quotation marks. Words not quoted must remain outside the quotation marks.

"If it is hot on Sunday," she said, "we will go to the beach."

2. An indirect quote must not be enclosed by quotation marks.

She said that we might go to the beach on Sunday.

3. When a multiple-paragraph passage is quoted, each paragraph of the quotation must begin with

quotation marks, but ending quotation marks are used only at the end of the last quoted paragraph.

4. A period always goes inside the quotation marks, whether the quotation marks are used to denote quoted material, to set off titles—such as chapters in a book or titles of short stories—or to isolate words used in a special sense.

> Jane explained, "The house is just around the corner."

> The first chapter of *The Andromeda Strain* is entitled "The Country of Lost Borders."

> Pornography is sold under the euphemism "adult books."

5. A comma always goes inside the quotation marks.

> "I really must go home," said the dinner guest.

> If your skills have become "rusty," you must study before you apply for the job.

> Three stories in Kurt Vonnegut's *Welcome to the Monkey House* are "Harrison Bergeron," "Next Door," and "Epicac."

6. A question mark goes inside the quotation marks if it is part of the quotation. If the whole

sentence containing the quotation is a question, the question mark goes outside the quotation marks.

He asked, "Was the airplane on time?"

What did you really mean when you said, "I do"?

7. An exclamation mark goes inside the quotation marks if the quoted words are an exclamation, outside if the entire sentence including the quotation is an exclamation.

The sentry shouted, "Drop your gun!"

Save us from our "friends"!

8. A colon and a semicolon always go outside the quotation marks.

He said, "War is destructive"; she added, "peace is constructive."

9. Words used in an unusual way may be placed inside quotation marks.

A surfer who "hangs ten" is performing a tricky maneuver on a surfboard.

10. A quotation within a quotation may be set apart by single quotes (apostrophes).

George said, "The philosophy 'I think, therefore I am' may be attributed to Descartes."

SEMICOLON

Always single-space after a semicolon.

1. A semicolon may be used to join two short, related independent clauses.

   > Anne is working at the front desk on Monday; Pedro will take over on Tuesday.

   Two independent clauses must be joined by a conjunction (and comma) or by a semicolon (or colon) or must be written as two sentences. A semicolon never precedes a coordinating conjunction. The same two clauses may be written:

   > Autumn had come to our mountain home, and the trees were almost bare. (Use a comma when conjoining longer independent clauses.)

   > Autumn had come to our mountain home; the trees were almost bare. (Use a semicolon when conjoining two independent clauses.)

   > Autumn had come to our mountain home. The trees were almost bare.

2. A semicolon may be used to join two independent clauses which are connected by an adverb such as *however, therefore, otherwise,* or *nevertheless.* The adverb must be followed by a comma.

We went to the track; however, the race was rained out.

You may use a semicolon to join one clause with the next; however, you will not be incorrect if you choose to write two separate sentences.

We went to the track. However, the race was rained out.

If you are uncertain how to use the semicolon to connect independent clauses, write two sentences instead.

3. A semicolon should be used to separate a series of phrases or clauses, especially when those phrases and clauses contain commas.

The old gentleman's heirs were Margaret Whitlock, his half-sister; James Bagley, the butler; William Frame, companion to his late cousin, Robert Bone; and his favorite charity, the Salvation Army.

CAPITALIZATION

1. Capitalize the first word of a complete sentence.

   Your favorite television program is on now.

2. Capitalize the first word of a quoted sentence.

   The bookkeeper said, "Please identify your personal long-distance phone calls."

   Do *not* capitalize the first word within quotation marks if it does not begin a complete sentence.

   "I tore my stocking," she told us, "because the drawer was left open."

3. Capitalize the letter *I* when it stands alone.

4. Capitalize the first letter of the first, last, and each important word in the title of a book, play, article, etc.

   "The Mystery of the Green Ghost"

   A Night at the Opera

5. Capitalize a title when it is used with the name of a person, group, or document.

   > Senator Jane Doe is a leading figure in the Republican Party.

   Do *not* capitalize the same type of title when it does not make a specific reference.

   > The congressman is a liberal; his opponent is a conservative.

   > It would be useful for our club to write a constitution.

6. Capitalize days of the week, months of the year, and holidays, but do *not* capitalize the seasons.

   > Labor Day, the last holiday of the summer, falls on the first Monday in September.

7. Capitalize the points of the compass only when referring to a specific place or region.

   > Many retired persons spend the winter in the South.

   Do not capitalize the points of the compass when they refer to a direction.

   > The birds were flying south.

8. The only school subjects that are regularly capitalized are languages and specific place names used as modifiers.

Next year we will offer French, English literature, biology, mathematics, European history, and ancient philosophy.

9. A noun not regularly capitalized should be capitalized when it is used as part of a proper name.

Yesterday I visited Uncle Fester, my favorite uncle.

10. In a letter, capitalize all titles in the address and closing.

Mr. John Jones, President

Mary Smith, Chairman of the Board

Capitalize the first and last words, titles, and proper names in the salutation.

Dear Dr. Williams,

My dear Sir:

Capitalize only the first word in a complimentary closing.

Very truly yours,

11. Capitalize all proper names—including, but not limited to, the names of people (*John F. Smith*); buildings (*World Trade Center*); events (*Veterans Day*); places (*Panama*) and words formed using those places (*Panamanian*); organizations

(*The United Fund*); and words referring to a sole God (*Allah*).

Some words derived from proper names have lost their proper-name meaning and have acquired an independent meaning in a different context. Many of these words are no longer capitalized. Below is a list of some lowercased derivatives of proper names. Consult a dictionary if in doubt.

argyle wool	artesian well
bourbon whisky	bowie knife
china clay	chinook salmon
degaussing apparatus	delftware
fedora hat	frankfurter
japan varnish	jersey fabric
knickerbocker	kraft paper
lyonnaise potatoes	macadamized road
osnaburg cloth	oxford cloth
petri dish	philistinism
surah silk	timothy grass
zeppelin	

NUMBERS

SPELLED OUT

1. Two general rules apply to expressing numbers. One or the other should be followed consistently within a piece of writing.

   a. Spell out numbers through nine; use figures from 10 on.

      two people

      three times as large

      14 recommendations

   b. Spell out numbers through ninety-nine; use figures from 100 on.

      eighty-six apples

      forty people

      163 pages

2. Any number that begins a sentence:

   Nineteen eighty-three was the company's best year.

   Two hundred forty workers were hired.

3. Centuries, round numbers, and indefinite expressions:

   hundreds of men

   the early seventies, *but* the 1890s, mid-1964

   the nineteenth century

4. Large numbers in very formal writing such as legal work. Use the following forms as models:

   sixteen hundred and twenty

   exactly four thousand

   fifty-two thousand one hundred and ninety-five

   nineteen hundred and eighty-four

5. Fractions standing alone or followed by *of a* or *of an:*

   one-half inch

   three-fourths of a pie

   one-third of an acre

6. Ordinal numbers less than one hundred:

> twentieth century
>
> eighty-second congress
>
> Fifth Fleet
>
> Twelfth Avenue

EXPRESSED IN FIGURES

1. Numbers over one hundred within ordinary text:

> Enrollment reached 16,847.
>
> 952 ballots   101 districts

2. All numbers in tabular material.

3. Measurements of physical properties in scientific or technical writing, and any number used with a symbol or abbreviated unit of measurement:

> 20/20 vision   43 mm
>
> 32° F   1 yd.
>
> 17 1/2"   8:30 A.M.

4. Serial numbers, including numbers designating the pages and other parts of a book:

   Bulletin 756

   pages 322–345

   diagram 4

5. Years:

   53 B.C.   1925

6. Fractions that would be awkward if spelled out:

   8 $\frac{1}{2}$-by-11-inch bond

7. Decimal fractions and percentages:

   10.5 percent return $83.95

   a grade point average of 3.42

8. All numbers referring to the same category in a single passage if the largest is over one hundred:

   Of the 137 delegates at the twelve o'clock meeting, only 9 opposed the plan.

LARGE NUMBERS

Large numbers are usually expressed in figures; however, numbers from a million up which end in four or more zeros may be expressed in text by combining figures and words. In the examples that follow, preference is based on the ease with which the number can be grasped in reading.

Figures:	299,789,655
Preferred:	299,789,655

Figures:	$12,000,000
Preferred:	$12 million
Acceptable:	12 million dollars

Figures:	3,250,000
Preferred:	3.25 million
Acceptable:	3 1/4 million
Or:	three and one-fourth million
Or:	three and one-quarter million

Figures:	9,000,000 to 1,000,000,000
Preferred:	9 million to 1 billion
Acceptable:	nine million to one billion

ROMAN NUMERALS

It is generally preferable to use Arabic numbers, as they are more easily understood than Roman numerals.

A repeated letter repeats its value; a letter placed after one of greater value adds to it; a letter placed before one of greater value subtracts from it; a dashline over a letter denotes multiplied by 1,000.

I	1	XXX	30	DC	600
II	2	XL	40	DCC	700
III	3	L	50	DCCC	800
IV	4	LX	60	CM	900
V	5	LXX	70	M	1,000
VI.	6	LXXX	80	MD	1,500
VII	7	XC	90	MM	2,000
VIII	8	C	100	MMM	3,000
IX	9	CL	150	$M\overline{V}$	4,000
X	10	CC	200	$\overline{V}$	5,000
XV	15	CCC	300	$\overline{M}$	1,000,000
XIX	19	CD	400		
XX	20	D	500		

Dates

MDC	1600	MCMXL	1940
MDCC	1700	MCML	1950
MDCCC	1800	MCMLX	1960
MCM or MDCCCC	1900	MCMLXX	1970
		MCMLXXX	1980
MCMX	1910	MCMXC	1990
MCMXX	1920	MM	2000
MCMXXX	1930		

COMPOUND WORDS

A compound is a union of two or more words; it conveys a unit idea that is not as clearly or quickly conveyed by the component words in unconnected succession. Compounds may be spelled open (with a space), solid (with no space), or with a hyphen.

Since ours is a fluid, changing language, the rules that follow can only provide guidelines to common practice. Word forms constantly undergo modification. Two-word forms often acquire the hyphen first and are later printed solid. Sometimes the transition is from open to solid, bypassing the hyphenated form. The trend recently has been toward solid spellings; for instance, the once-common spellings *life style* and *life-style* have now generally given way to *lifestyle*. Check a current, reliable dictionary for guidance.

GENERAL RULES

1. In general, omit the hyphen when words appear in regular order and the omission causes no ambiguity in sense or sound.

banking hours	real estate	patent right
blood pressure	fellow citizen	rock candy
book value	living costs	training ship
census taker	palm oil	violin teacher

2. Words are usually combined to express a literal or nonliteral (figurative) unit idea that would not be as clearly expressed in unconnected succession.

afterglow	forget-me-not	right-handed
bookkeeping	gentleman	whitewash
cupboard	newsprint	eye-opener

3. Unless otherwise indicated, a derivative of a compound, that is, a compound which is derived from another compound, retains the solid or hyphenated form of the original compound.

coldbloodedness	praiseworthiness
footnoting	railroader
ill-advisable	X-rayer
outlawry	Y-shaped

4. Except after the short prefixes *co, de, pre, pro,* and *re,* which are generally typed solid, a hyphen is used to avoid doubling the same vowel or tripling the same consonant.

cooperation	*but* semi-independent
semiannual	thimble-eye
preexisting	ultra-atomic
antiaircraft	shell-like

Solid Compounds

1. Consider solid (as one word) two nouns that form a third when the compound has only one primary accent, especially when the prefixed noun consists of only one syllable or when one of the elements loses its original accent.

airship	cupboard	footnote
bathroom	dressmaker	locksmith
bookseller	fishmonger	workman

2. Consider solid a noun consisting of a short verb and a terminal adverb, except when the use of the solid form would interfere with comprehension.

blowout	runoff
flareback	setup
giveaway	throwaway
hangover	*but* cut-in
makeready	run-in
pickup	tie-in

3. Compounds beginning with the following nouns are usually considered solid.

book(end)	mill(work)	snow(fall)
eye	play	way
horse	school	wood
house	shop	work

4. Compounds ending in the following are usually considered solid, especially when the prefixed word consists of one syllable.

(blue)berry	(bird)brained	(bond)holder
blossom	bush	house
boat	fish	keeper
book	flower	keeping
borne	grower	light
bound	hearted	like
maker	room	wise
making	shop	woman
man	smith	wood
master	stone	work
mate	store	worker

mill	tail	working
mistress	tight	worm
monger	time (*not* clock)	wort
owner	ward	writer
piece	way	writing
power	weed	yard
proof	wide	

5. Consider solid *any, every, no,* and *some* when combined with *body, thing,* and *where.* When *one* is the second element, print as two words if meaning a single or particular person or thing. To avoid mispronunciation, print *no one* as two words at all times.

6. Consider solid compound personal pronouns.

herself	oneself	thyself
himself	ourselves	yourself
itself	themselves	yourselves
myself		

7. Consider solid compass directions consisting of two points, but use a hyphen after the first point when three points are combined.

northeast	north-northwest
southwest	south-southeast

Unit Modifiers

1. Except as indicated in the other rules in this chapter, type a hyphen between words, or abbreviations and words, combined to form a unit modifier immediately preceding the word modified. This applies particularly to combinations in which the second element is a present or past participle.

Baltimore-Washington road

collective-bargaining talks

drought-stricken area

English-speaking nation

fire-tested material

German-English descent

hard-of-hearing class

large-scale project

most-favored-nation clause

multiple-purpose uses

no-par-value stock

part-time personnel

rust-resistant covering

service-connected disability

tool-and-die maker

U.S.-owned property

2. Where meaning is clear and readability is not aided, it is not necessary to use a hyphen to form a temporary (or made) compound. Restraint should be exercised in forming unnecessary combinations of words used in normal sequence.

atomic energy power

bituminous coal industry

child welfare plan

durable goods industry

flood control study

high school student; elementary school grade

income tax form

land bank loan

mutual security funds

national defense appropriation

parcel post delivery

real estate tax

small businessman

but   no-growth policy (readability aided); *not* no growth policy

3. When the second element is a present or past participle and the unit modifier does not immediately precede the thing modified, omit the hyphen.

The effects were far reaching.

The shale was oil bearing.

These cars are higher priced.

4. Use without a hyphen a two-word modifier when the first element is a comparative or superlative.

better drained soil

higher level decision

larger sized dress

but   lowercase, uppercase type (printing)

upperclassman

bestseller (noun)

lighter-than-air craft

higher-than-market price

5. Do not use a hyphen in a two-word unit modifier when the first element is an adverb ending in -*ly*. Do not use hyphens in a three-word unit modifier the first two elements of which are adverbs.

> eagerly awaited moment
>
> unusually well preserved specimen
>
> very well defined usage
>
> longer than usual lunch period
>
> *but* still-new car, because *still* is an adverb and *new* is an adjective
>
>   ever-rising flood
>
>   still-lingering doubt
>
>   well-known lawyer
>
>   well-kept farm

6. Proper nouns used as unit modifiers—either in their basic or derived form—retain their original form, but the hyphen is used after combining forms of proper nouns.

> Latin American countries
>
> North Carolina roads
>
> a Mexican American

South American trade

but Winston-Salem festival

Washington-Wilkes–Barre route

African-American program

Anglo-Saxon period

7. Do not confuse a modifier with the word it modifies.

prudent stockholder

competent shoemaker

gallant serviceman

average taxpayer

well-trained schoolteacher

stockownership

wooden-shoe maker

service men and women

American-flag ship

8. Where two or more hyphenated compounds have a common basic element and this element is omitted in all but the last term, the hyphens are retained.

two- to three-ton trucks

8-, 10-, and 16-foot boards

moss- and ivy-covered walls, *not* moss and
ivy-covered walls

but twofold or threefold, *not* two or threefold

goat, sheep, and calf skins, *not* goat, sheep,
and calfskins

9. Omit the hyphen in a unit modifier containing a
   letter or numeral as its second element.

   abstract B pages   grade A milk

   article 3 provisions   class II railroad

Prefixes, Suffixes, and Combining Forms

1. Compounds formed with prefixes and suffixes
   are typed solid, except as indicated elsewhere.

*after*birth	*Anglo*mania	*ante*date
*anti*slavery	*bi*weekly	*by*law
*circum*navigation	*cis*alpine	clock*wise*
cover*age*	*de*cry	*demi*tasse
*ex*communicate	*extra*curricular	*fore*tell
geo*graphy*	home*stead*	*hyper*sensitive
*hypo*center	*in*bound	*infra*red

*intro*vert	*iso*metric	kilo*gram*
lone*some*	man*hood*	*macro*biotics
*multi*color	*neo*phyte	*non*neutral
north*ward*	*off*set	oper*ate*
*pan*cosmic	*para*centric	partner*ship*
*pseudo*science	pump*kin*	*ree*nact
retro*spect*	self*ish*	*semi*official
*super*market	*thermo*couple	*trans*onic
*ultra*violet	*under*coat	*un*necessary

2. Consider solid words ending in *like,* but use a hyphen to avoid tripling a consonant or when the first element is a proper name.

lifelike	*but* bell-like
lilylike	Florida-like
girllike	Truman-like

3. Use a hyphen or hyphens to prevent mispronunciation, to insure a definite accent on each element of the compound, or to avoid ambiguity.

anti-hog-cholera serum	re-cover (cover again)
co-op	re-sort (sort again)

| mid-ice | re-treat (treat again) |
| non-civil-service position | un-ionized |

non-tumor-bearing tissue

4. Use with a hyphen the prefixes *ex, self,* and *quasi.*

ex-governor	quasi-academic
ex-serviceman	quasi-argument
ex-trader	quasi-corporate
ex-vice president	quasi-young
self-control	*but* selfhood
self-educated	selfsame

5. Unless usage demands otherwise, use a hyphen to join a prefix or combining form to a capitalized word. (The hyphen is retained in words of this class set in caps.)

anti-Arab	pro-British
un-American	*but* nongovernmental
non-Government	overanglicize
post-World War II	*or* transatlantic
post-Second World War	

6. The adjectives *elect* and *designate,* as the last element of a title, require a hyphen.

> president-elect   ambassador-designate
>
> mayor-elect   minister-designate

Numerical, Scientific, and Technical Compounds

1. Do not type a hyphen in scientific terms (names of chemicals, diseases, animals, insects, plants) used as unit modifiers if no hyphen appears in their original form.

> carbon monoxide poisoning
>
> guinea pig raising
>
> methyl bromide solution
>
> *but*   screw-worm raising
>
> > Russian-olive plantings
> >
> > white-pine weevil

2. Chemical elements used in combination with figures use a hyphen, except with superior figures.

> polonium-210
>
> uranium-235; *but* U^{225}; Sr^{90}; $_{92}U^{234}$
>
> Freon-12

3. Use a hyphen between the elements of technical compound units of measurement.

    candle-hour   light-year

    horsepower-hour   passenger-mile

    kilowatt-hour

Improvised Compounds

1. Use with a hyphen the elements of an improvised compound.

    blue-pencil (v.)

    18-year-old (n.)

    first-come-first-served basis

  but a basis of first come, first served

        easy come, easy go

2. Use a hyphen to join a single capital letter to a noun or participle.

    H-bomb   X-raying

    I-beam   T-shaped

    V-necked   U-boat

USAGE

This section is a guide to the correct use of words and phrases that are frequently misused.

abbreviate—means *to shorten by omitting*.
abridge—means *to shorten by condensing*.
New York is *abbreviated* to NY, Tennessee to TN.
In order to save time in the reading, the report was *abridged*.

ability—means a *developed, actual* power.
capacity—means an *undeveloped, potential* power.
He now has fair writing *ability,* but additional courses in college will develop his *capacity* beyond the average level.

above—Avoid *above* except in business forms where it may be used in reference to a preceding part of the text.
In normal writing use *foregoing* or *preceding,* instead of *above.*
Unacceptable: The *above* books are available in the library.
Acceptable: The *above* prices are subject to change without notice.

accede—means *to agree with.*

concede—means *to yield,* but not necessarily in agreement.

exceed—means *to be more than.*

We *accede* to your request for more evidence.

The candidate *conceded* the victory to his opponent.

My expenses often *exceed* my income.

accept—means *to take when offered.*

except—means *excluding.* (preposition)

except—means *to leave out.* (verb)

I *accept* the proposition that all men are created equal.

All eighteen-year-olds *except* seniors will be called.

The final report will *except* all data that doesn't conform to standards.

access—means *availability.*

excess—means *too much.*

The lawyer was given *access* to the grand jury records.

Their expenditures this month are far in *excess* of their income.

in accord with—means in agreement with *a person.*

I am *in accord with* you about this.

in accordance with—means in agreement with a *thing.*

The police officer acted *in accordance with* the law.

acoustics—when used as a singular noun means the *science* of sound.
Acoustics is a subdivision of physics.

acoustics—when used as a plural noun denotes the *qualities* of sound.
The *acoustics* of Carnegie Hall are incomparable.

acquiesce in—means *to accept,* with or without objection.
Although there is some doubt about your plan, I *acquiesce in* its adoption.

ad—is a colloquial, clipped form for *advertisement;* it is not to be used in formal writing. Other colloquial words of this type are *exam (examination), auto (automobile), lab (laboratory), demo (demonstration),* and *dorm (dormitory).*

adapt—means *to adjust* or *change.*
adopt—means to *take as one's own.*
adept—means *skillful.*
Children can *adapt* to changing conditions very easily.
The war orphan was *adopted* by the general and his wife.
Proper instruction makes children *adept* in various games.

addicted to —means *accustomed to by strong habit*.
subject to—means *exposed to* or *liable to*.
> People *addicted to* drugs or alcohol need constant medical care.
> The coast of Wales is *subject to* extremely heavy fogs.

addition—means *the act or process of adding*.
edition—means *a printing of a publication*.
> In *addition* to a dictionary, she always used a thesaurus.
> The first *edition* of Shakespeare's plays appeared in 1623.

advantage—means *a superior position*.
benefit—means *a favor conferred or earned* (as a profit).
> He had an *advantage* in experience over his opponent.
> The rules were changed for her *benefit*.
> NOTE: To *take* advantage *of*, to *have* an advantage *over*.

adverse—means *unfavorable*.
averse—means *disliking* or *reluctant*.
> He took the *adverse* decision in poor spirit.
> Many students are *averse* to criticism by their classmates.

affect—means *to influence* or *to pretend*. (a verb)
effect—means *an influence* or *result*. (a noun)
effect—means *to bring about*. (a verb)
>Your education must *affect* your future.
>He *affected* a great love for opera, though in fact it bored him.
>The *effect* of the last war is still being felt.
>A diploma *effected* a tremendous change in his attitude.

affection—means *feeling*.
affectation—means *pose* or *artificial behavior*.
>Alumni often develop a strong *affection* for their former schools.
>The *affectation* of a Harvard accent is no guarantee of success.

affinity—means an *attraction to a person or thing*.
infinity—means an *unlimited time, space, or quantity*.
>She has an *affinity* for men with beards.
>It is impossible to visualize an *infinity* of anything.

after—is unnecessary with the past participle.
>Not: *After having checked* the timetable, she left.
>But: *Having checked* the timetable, she left.

aggravate—means *to make worse*.
exasperate—means *to irritate* or *annoy*.

Her cold was *aggravated* by faulty medication.
His inability to make a quick recovery *exasperated* him exceedingly.

ain't—is an unacceptable contraction for *am not, are not,* or *is not.*

aisle—is *a passageway* between seats.
isle—is a *small island.*

alibi—is an explanation on *the basis of being in another place.*
excuse—is an explanation on *any basis.*
The *alibi* offered at the trial was that he was twenty miles away from the scene of the crime.
His *excuse* for failing on the test was that he was sick.

alimentary—refers to *the process of nutrition.*
elementary—means *primary.*
The *alimentary* canal includes the stomach and the intestines.
Elementary education is the foundation of all human development.

all ready—means *everybody or everything ready.*
already—means *previously.*
They were *all ready* to write when the teacher arrived.

They had *already* begun writing when the teacher arrived.

all-round—means *versatile* or *general.*
all around—means *all over a given area.*
Rafer Johnson, decathlon champion, is an *all-round* athlete.
The police were scouring for evidence for miles *all around.*

all together—means *everybody or everything together.*
altogether—means *completely.*
The boys and girls sang *all together.*
This was *altogether* strange for a person of her age.

all ways—means *in every possible way.*
always—means *at all times.*
She was in *all ways* acceptable to the voters.
Their reputation had *always* been spotless.

allow—means *to give permission.*
Acceptable: The teacher *allows* adequate time for study in class.
Unacceptable: I *allow* I haven't ever seen anything like this.

allude—means *to make an indirect reference to.*
elude—means *to escape from.*
> Only incidentally does Coleridge *allude* to Shakespeare's puns.
> It is almost impossible for one to *elude* tax collectors.

allusion—means *an indirect reference.*
illusion—means *a deception of the eye or mind.*
> The student made *allusions* to his teacher's habits.
> *Illusions* of the mind, unlike those of the eye, cannot be corrected with glasses.

alongside of—means *side by side with.*
alongside—means *parallel to the side.*
> Bill stood *alongside of* Henry.
> Park the car *alongside* the curb.

allot—means *apportion.*
alot—is an unacceptable spelling for *a lot. A lot,* meaning *very much,* should be avoided in formal writing.
> They *allotted* the prize money equally among the winners.
> Not: We like the proposal *a lot.*
> But: We like the proposal *very much.*

alumnus—means *a male graduate*.

alumna—means *a female graduate*.

With the granting of the diploma, he became an *alumnus* of the school.

She is an *alumna* of Hunter College.

NOTE: The masculine plural form of *alumnus* is *alumni* (*-ni* rhymes with *hi*). The feminine plural form is *alumnae* (*-ae* rhymes with *key*). Use *alumni* when referring to both men and women.

amend—means *to correct*.

emend—means *to correct a literary work; to edit*.

Our Constitution, as *amended* by the Bill of Rights, was finally ratified.

Before publication, several chapters of the book had to be *emended*.

among—is used with *more than two persons or things*.

NOTE: *Amongst* should be avoided.

between—is used with *two persons or things*.

The inheritance was equally divided *among* the four children.

The business, however, was divided *between* the oldest and the youngest one.

amount—applies to quantities *that cannot be counted one by one*.

number—applies to quantities *that can be counted one by one*.

A large *amount* of grain was delivered to the store.
A large *number* of bags were delivered.

and etc.—is unacceptable for *etc.*, a Latin abbreviation meaning *and other things.* It is best to use *etc.* only when you are sure your reader will understand what other items or kinds of items you are referring to—for instance, when referring to a list of things already mentioned in full. Beware of *etc.* as a cover for vague or sloppy thinking.

annual—means *yearly.*
biannual and **semiannual**—mean *twice a year.*
biennial—means *once in two years, every two years.*
>The Saint Patrick's Day parade is an *annual* event in New York city.
>Some schools have *biannual* promotion, in January and June.
>The *biennial* election of Congressmen is held in the even numbered years.

another such—is *acceptable.*
such another—is *unacceptable.*
>*Another such* error may lead to legal prosecution.
>After his illness, he seemed *quite another* (**not** *such another*) person from what he had been.

ante—is a prefix meaning *before*.

anti—is a prefix meaning *against*.

The *ante*chamber is the room just before the main room.

An *anti*fascist is one who is opposed to fascists.

anxious—means *worried*.

eager—means *keenly desirous*.

We were *anxious* about our first airplane flight.

We are *eager* to fly again.

Any other—indicates a comparison. Do not use *any* by itself for a comparison.

He likes France better than *any other* country.

anywheres—is *unacceptable*.

anywhere—is *acceptable*.

We can't find it *anywhere*.

Similarly, use *nowhere* (**not** *nowheres*) and *somewhere* (**not** *somewheres*).

appraise—means *to set a value*.

apprise—means *to inform*.

The jeweler *appraised* the diamond at a very high value.

We were *apprised* of their arrival by the honking of the car horn.

apprehend—means to *catch the meaning of something*.

comprehend—means *to understand a thing completely*.

At first I didn't *apprehend* his true intent.

It is often difficult to *comprehend* the Euclidean postulates.

NOTE: *Apprehend* may also mean *to take into custody*.

The sheriff succeeded in *apprehending* the rustler.

apt—suggests *habitual behavior*.

likely—suggests *probable behavior*.

liable—suggests an *exposure to something harmful*.

Children are *apt* to be rather lazy in the morning.

A cat, if annoyed, is *likely* to scratch.

Cheating on a test may make one *liable* to expulsion from school.

argue—means *to prove something by logical methods*.

quarrel—means *to dispute without reason or logic*.

The opposing lawyers *argued* before the judge.

The lawyers became emotional and *quarreled*.

artisan—means *mechanic* or *craftsman*.

artist—means *one who practices the fine arts*.

Many *artisans* participated in the building of the Sistine Chapel.

The basic design, however, was prepared by the *artist* Michelangelo.

as—(used as a conjunction) is followed by a verb.
like—(used as a preposition) is not followed by a verb.
Do *as* I do, not *as* I say.
Try not to behave *like* a child.
Unacceptable: He acts *like* I do.

as good as—should be used *for comparisons only*.
This motel is *as good as* the next one.
Do not use *as good as* to mean *practically*.
Unacceptable: They *as good as* promised us a place in the hall.
Acceptable: They *practically* promised us a place in the hall.

as if—is correctly used in the expression, "He talked *as if* his jaw hurt him."
Unacceptable: "He talked *like* his jaw hurt him."

as per—is poor usage for *according to* or *in accordance with*.
He assembled the bicycle *in accordance with* (**not** *as per*) the directions.

as to whether—is *unacceptable*. *Whether* includes
the unnecessary words *as to*.
I don't know *whether* it is going to rain.

ascent—is *the act of rising*.
assent—means *approval*.
The *ascent* to the top of the mountain was perilous.
Congress gave its *assent* to the President's emergency directive.

assay—means *to try* or *experiment*.
essay—means *to make an intellectual effort*.
We shall *assay* the ascent of the mountain
tomorrow.
Why not *essay* a description of the mountain in
composition?

astonish—means *to strike with sudden wonder*.
surprise—means *to catch unaware*.
The extreme violence of the hurricane *astonished*
everybody.
A heat wave in January would *surprise* us.

at—should be avoided where it does not contribute
to the meaning.
Acceptable: Where shall I meet you?
Unacceptable: Where shall we meet *at*?
at about—should not be used for *about*.
The group will arrive *about* noon.

attend to—means *to take care of.*
tend to—means *to be inclined to.*
> One of the clerks will *attend to* my mail in my
> absence.
> Lazy people *tend to* lack ambition.

audience—means *a group of listeners.*
spectators—refers to *a group of watchers.*
> Leonard Bernstein conducted a concert for the
> school *audience.*
> The slow baseball game bored the *spectators.*
> NOTE: A group that both watches and listens is
> called an *audience.*

average—means *conforming to norms or standards.*
ordinary—means *usual, customary,* or *without dis-
tinction.*
> A book of about 300 pages is of *average* length.
> The contents of the book were rather *ordinary.*

back—should **not** be used with such words as *refer*
and *return* since the prefix *re-* means *back.*
> *Refer* to the text if you have difficulty recalling
> the facts.
balance—meaning *remainder,* is *acceptable* only in
commercial usage. Use *remainder* or *rest* otherwise.
> Even after the withdrawal, his bank *balance* was
> considerable.

Three of the students voted for John; the *rest* voted
   for Jim.

bazaar—is a *marketplace* or a *fair*.
bizarre—means *odd* or *strange*.
   We are going to the *bazaar* to buy things.
   He dresses in a *bizarre* manner.

being that—is *unacceptable* for *since* or *because*.
   Acceptable: Since you have come a long way, why
      not remain here for the night.

berth—is a *resting place*.
birth—means *the beginning of life*.
   The new liner was given a wide *berth* in the harbor.
   She was a fortunate woman from *birth*.

beside—means *close to*.
besides—means *in addition*.
   He lived *beside* the stream.
   He found wild flowers and weeds *besides*.

better—means *recovering*.
well—means *completely recovered*.
   Ivan is *better* now than he was a week ago.
   In a few more weeks, he will be *well*.

both—means *two considered together*.
each—means *one of two or more*.

Both of the applicants qualified for the position.
Each applicant was given a generous reference.

bouillon—is a *soup*.
bullion—means *gold* or *silver* in the form of bars.
   This restaurant serves tasty *bouillon*.
   A mint makes coins out of *bullion*.

breath—means an *intake of air.*
breathe—means *to draw air in and give it out.*
breadth—means *width.*
   Before you dive in, take a very deep *breath*.
   It is impossible *to breathe* under water.
   In a square, the *breadth* is equal to the length.

bridal—means *of a wedding.*
bridle—means to *hold back.*
   The *bridal* party was late to the church.
   You must learn to *bridle* your temper.

bring—means *to carry toward the person who is speaking.*
take—means *to carry away from the speaker.*
   Bring the books here.
   Take your raincoat with you when you go out.

broach—means *to mention for the first time.*
brooch—means an *ornament* for clothing.

At the meeting, one of the speakers *broached* the
question of salary increases.
The model was wearing an expensive *brooch*.

bunch—refers to *things*.
group—refers to *persons* or *things*.
This looks like a delicious *bunch* of bananas.
What a well-behaved *group* of children!
NOTE: The colloquial use of *bunch* applied to
persons should be avoided.

burst—is acceptable for broke.
bust—is unacceptable for broke (or broken).
Acceptable: The balloon burst.
Unacceptable: My pen is busted.

business—is sometimes incorrectly used for *work*.
Unacceptable: I went to *business* very late today.
Acceptable: He owns a thriving *business*.

but—should **not** be used after the expression *cannot help*.
Acceptable: One *cannot help noticing* the errors.
Unacceptable: One *cannot help but* notice . . .

byword—is *a pet expression*.
password—is *a secret word uttered to gain passage*.
In ancient Greece, truth and beauty were *bywords*.
The sentry asked the scout for the *password*.

calculate—means *to determine mathematically*. It does **not** mean *to think*.

Some students still know how to *calculate* on an abacus.

Unacceptable: I *calculate* it's going to rain.

calendar—is *a system of time*.
calender—is *a smoothing and glazing machine*.
colander—is *a kind of sieve*.

In this part of the world, most people prefer the twelve-month *calendar*.

In ceramic work, the potting wheel and the *calender* are indispensable.

Vegetables should be washed in a *colander* before cooking.

Calvary—is *the name of the place of the Crucifixion*.
cavalry—is a *military unit on horseback*.

Calvary and Gethsemane are place-names in the Bible.

Most of our modern *cavalry* is now motorized.

can—means *physically able*.
may—implies *permission*.

I *can* lift this chair over my head.

You *may* leave after you finish your work.

cannon—is a *gun* for heavy firing.
canon—is a *rule* or *law,* usually of a church.

Don't remain near the *cannon* when it is being
  fired.
Churchgoers are expected to observe the *canons*.

cannot help—must be followed by an *-ing* form.
  We cannot help *feeling* (**not** *feel*) distressed about
    this.
  NOTE: *cannot help but* is unacceptable.

can't hardly—is a double negative. It is *unacceptable*.
  The child *can hardly* walk in those shoes.

capital—is *the city* or *money*.
capitol—is *the building*.
  Paris is the *capital* of France.
  The *Capitol* in Washington is occupied by the
    Congress. (The Washington *Capitol* is capi-
    talized.)
  NOTE: *capital* also means wealth.

catalog—is a *systematic list*. (also **catalogue**)
category—is a *class* of things.
  The item is precisely described in the sales *catalog*.
  A trowel is included in the *category* of farm tools.

cease—means *to end*.
seize—means *to take hold of*.

Will you please *cease* making those sounds?
Seize the cat as it rounds the corner.

censer—is *a container which holds burning incense.*
censor—means *to examine for the purpose of judging moral aspects.*
censure—means *to find fault with.*
> One often finds a *censer* in church.
> The government *censors* films in some countries.
> She *censured* her husband for coming home late.

center around—is *unacceptable.* Use *center in* or *center on.*
> The maximum power was *centered in* the nuclear reactor.
> All attention was *centered on* the launching pad.

certainly—is an *adverb.*
sure—is an *adjective.*
> He was *certainly* learning fast.
> *Colloquial:* He *sure* was learning fast.

cession—means *a yielding.*
session—means *a meeting.*
> The *cession* of a piece of territory could have avoided the war.
> The legislative *session* lasted three months.

childish—means *silly, immature*.
childlike—means *innocent, unspoiled*.
> Pouting appears *childish* in an adult.
> His *childlike* appreciation of art gave him great
> pleasure.

choice—means *a selection*.
choose—means *to select*.
chose—means *selected*.
> My *choice* for a career is teaching.
> We may *choose* our own leader.
> I finally *chose* teaching for a career.

cite—means *to quote*.
sight—means *seeing*.
site—means *a place for a building*.
> He was fond of *citing* from the Scriptures.
> The *sight* of the wreck was appalling.
> The Board of Education is seeking a *site* for the
> new school.

climate—is the average weather *over a period of*
many years.
weather—is the *hour by hour* or *day by day* condition of the atmosphere.
> He likes the *climate* of California better than that
> of New York.
> The *weather* is sometimes hard to predict.

coarse—means *vulgar* or *harsh*.

course—means a *path* or a *subject of study*.

He was shunned because of his *coarse* behavior.

The ship took its usual *course*.

Which *course* in English are you taking?

comic—means *intentionally funny*.

comical—means *unintentionally funny*.

A clown is a *comic* figure.

The peculiar hat she wore gave her a *comical* appearance.

comma—is a *mark of punctuation*.

coma—(rhymes with *aroma*) means *a period of prolonged unconsciousness*.

A *comma* should never separate two complete sentences.

The accident put him into a *coma* lasting three days.

common—means *shared equally* by two or more.

mutual—means *interchanged*.

The town hall is the *common* pride of every citizen.

We can do business to our *mutual* profit and satisfaction.

compare to—means to liken to something *which has a different form*.

compare with—means to compare persons or things with each other *when they are of the same kind.*

contrast with—means to show the *difference between two things.*

A minister is sometimes *compared to* a shepherd.

Shakespeare's plays are often *compared with* those of Marlowe.

The writer *contrasted* the sensitivity of the dancer *with* the grossness of the pugilist.

complement—means *a completing part.*

compliment—is *an expression of admiration.*

His wit was a *complement* to her beauty.

He received many *compliments* on his valedictory speech.

comprehensible—means *understandable.*

comprehensive—means *including a great deal.*

Under the circumstances, your doubts were *comprehensible.*

Toynbee's *comprehensive* study of history covers many centuries.

comprise—means *to include.*

compose—means *to form the substance of.*

Toynbee's study of history *comprises* seven volumes.

Some modern novels are *composed* of as little as three chapters.

concur in—must be followed by *an action*.

concur with—must be followed by *a person*.

> I shall *concur in* the decision reached by the majority.
>
> I cannot *concur with* the chairman, however much I respect his opinion.

conducive to—means *leading to*.

conducive for—is *unacceptable*.

> Your proposals for compromise are *conducive to* a settlement of our disagreement.

conform to—means *to adapt oneself to*.

conform with—means *to be in harmony with*.

> Youngsters are inclined to *conform to* a group pattern.
>
> They feel it is dangerous not to *conform with* the rules of the group.

conscience—means *sense of right*.

conscientious—means *faithful*.

conscious—means *aware*.

> Man's *conscience* prevents him from becoming completely selfish.
>
> We value her because she is *conscientious*.
>
> The injured man was completely *conscious*.

considerable—is properly used *only as an adjective*, **not** as a noun.

Acceptable: The fraternal organization invested a *considerable* amount in government bonds.
Unacceptable: He lost *considerable* in the stock market.

consistently—means *in harmony.*
constantly—means *regularly, steadily.*
If you choose to give advice, act *consistently* with that advice.
Doctors *constantly* warn against overexertion.

consul—means *a government representative.*
council—means *an assembly which meets for deliberation.*
counsel—means *advice.*
Americans abroad should keep in touch with their *consuls.*
The City *Council* enacts local laws and regulations.
The defendant heeded the *counsel* of his friends.

contemptible—means *worthy of contempt.*
contemptuous—means *feeling contempt.*
His spying activities were *contemptible.*
It was plain to all that he was *contemptuous* of his co-workers.

continual—means happening *again and again at short intervals.*
continuous—means *without interruption.*

The teacher gave the class *continual* warnings.
Noah experienced *continuous* rain for forty days.

convenient to—should be followed by a *person*.
convenient for—should be followed by a *purpose*.
Will these plans be *convenient to* you?
You must agree that they are *convenient for* the
occasion.

copy—is *an imitation of an original work.* (not necessarily an exact imitation)
facsimile—is *an exact imitation of an original work.*
The counterfeiters made a crude *copy* of the
hundred-dollar bill.
The official government engraver, however,
prepared a *facsimile* of the bill.

core—means the *heart of something.*
corps—(pronounced like *core*) means *an organized
military body.*
corpse—means *a dead body.*
The *core* of the apple was rotten.
The *corps* consisted of three full-sized armies.
The *corpse* was quietly slipped overboard after a
brief service.

corespondent—is *a joint defendant in a divorce case.*
correspondent—is *one who communicates.*

The *corespondent* declared that he loved the other man's wife.

Max Frankel is a special *correspondent* for the New York Times.

corporeal—means *bodily as opposed to spiritual.*
corporal—means *bodily as it pertains to a person.*

Many believe that our *corporeal* existence changes to a spiritual one after death.

Corporal punishment is not recommended in modern schools.

could of—is unacceptable for *could have.* Similarly, avoid *should of, must of,* and *would of.*

Not: I *could of* won.

But: I *could have* won.

credible—means *believable.*
creditable—means *worthy of receiving praise.*
credulous—means *believing too easily.*

The pupil gave a *credible* explanation for his lateness.

Considering all the handicaps, he gave a *creditable* performance.

Politicians might prefer to address *credulous* people.

decease—means *death.*
disease—means *illness.*

His friend is *deceased*.
Leukemia is a deadly *disease*.

decent—means *suitable*.
descent—means *going down*.
dissent—means *disagreement*.
The *decent* thing to do is to admit your fault.
The *descent* into the cave was treacherous.
Two of the nine justices filed a *dissenting* opinion.

deduction—means *reasoning from the general* (laws or principles) *to the particular* (facts).
induction—means *reasoning from the particular* (facts) *to the general* (laws or principles).
All men are mortal. Since John is a man, he is mortal. (*deduction*)
There are 1,000 oranges in this truckload. I have examined 100 from various parts of the load and find them all of the same quality. I therefore conclude that the 1,000 oranges are of this quality. (*induction*)

deference—means *respect*.
difference—means *unlikeness*.
In *deference* to his memory, we did not play yesterday.
The *difference* between the two boys is unmistakable.

definite—means *clear, with set limits*.
definitive—means *final, decisive*.
> We would prefer a *definite* answer to our *definite* question.
> The dictionary is the *definitive* authority for word meanings.

deprecate—means *to disapprove*.
depreciate—means *to lower the value*.
> His classmates *deprecated* his discourtesy.
> The service station *depreciated* the value of our house.

desirable—means *that which is desired*.
desirous—means *desiring* or *wanting*.
> It was a most *desirable* position.
> She was *desirous* of obtaining it.

despise—means *to look down upon*.
detest—means *to hate*.
> Some wealthy persons *despise* the poor.
> I *detest* cold weather.

desert—(pronounced DEZ-ert) means *an arid area*.
desert—(pronounced di-ZERT) means *to abandon;* it is also *a reward or punishment*.
dessert—(pronounced di-ZERT) means *the final course of a meal*.

The Sahara is the world's most famous *desert*.
A husband must not *desert* his wife.
Execution was a just *desert* for his crime.
We had plum pudding for *dessert*.

device—means *a way to do something.* (a noun)
devise—means *to find the way.* (a verb)
  A hook is a good fishing *device*.
  Some fishermen prefer to *devise* other ways for
    catching fish.

differ from—is used when there is a difference *between things*.
differ with—is used when there is a difference *in opinion*.
  A coat *differs from* a cape.
  You have the right to *differ with* me on public
    affairs.

different from—is *acceptable.*
different than—is *unacceptable.*
  Acceptable: Jack is *different from* his brother.
  Unacceptable: Florida's climate is *different than*
    New York's climate.

discover—means *to find something already in existence.*
invent—means *to create something that never existed before.*

Pasteur *discovered* germs.
Whitney *invented* the cotton gin.

discreet—means *cautious*.
discrete—means *separate*.
> The employee was *discreet* in her comments about her employer.
> Since these two questions are *discrete,* you must provide two separate answers.

disinterested—means *impartial*.
uninterested—means *not interested*.
> The judge must always be a *disinterested* party in a trial.
> As an *uninterested* observer, he was inclined to yawn at times.

divers—(pronounced DI-vurz) means *several*.
diverse—(pronounced di-VERS) means *different*.
> The store had *divers* foodstuffs for sale.
> Many of the items were completely *diverse* from staple foods.

doubt that—is *acceptable*.
doubt whether—is *unacceptable*.
> *Acceptable:* I *doubt that* you will pass this term.
> *Unacceptable:* I *doubt whether* you will succeed.

doubtless—is *acceptable*.
doubtlessly—is *unacceptable*.
> *Acceptable:* You *doubtless* know your work; why, then, don't you pass?
> *Unacceptable:* He *doubtlessly* thinks that you can do the job well.

dual—means *relating to two*.
duel—means *a contest between two persons*.
> Dr. Jekyl had a *dual* personality.
> Alexander Hamilton was fatally injured in a *duel* with Aaron Burr.

each other—refers to *two persons*.
one another—may also refer to *more than two persons*.
> The two girls have known *each other* for many years.
> Several of the girls have known *one another* for many years.

economic—refers to the *subject of economics*.
economical—means *thrifty*.
> An *economic* discussion was held at the United Nations.
> A smart shopper is usually *economical*.

either . . . or—is used when referring to choices.
neither . . . nor—is the *negative* form.

Either you *or* I will win the election.
Neither Bill *nor* Ellen is expected to have a chance.

elegy—is a *mournful or melancholy poem.*
eulogy—is a *speech in praise of a deceased person.*
   Gray's "*Elegy* Written in a Country Churchyard"
   is a melancholy poem.
   The minister delivered the *eulogy.*

eligible—means *fit to be chosen.*
illegible—means *impossible to read* or *hard to read.*
   Not all persons are *eligible* to be President.
   His childish handwriting was *illegible.*

eliminate—means *to get rid of.*
illuminate—means *to supply with light.*
   Let us try to *eliminate* the unnecessary steps.
   Several lamps were needed to *illuminate* the
   corridor.

else—is superfluous in such expressions as the
   following:
   Unacceptable: We want *no one else* but you.
   Acceptable: We want *no one* but you.

emigrate—means *to leave one's country for another.*
immigrate—means *to enter another country.*
   The Norwegians *emigrated* to America in
   mid-1860.

Many of the Norwegian *immigrants* settled in the Midwest.

enclosed herewith—is *redundant*.
enclosed—is *acceptable*.
You will find *enclosed* one copy of our brochure.

endorse—means to write on the back of.
Acceptable: He endorsed the check.
Unacceptable: He endorsed the check on the back.

enormity—means *viciousness or great wickedness*.
enormousness—means *vastness*.
The *enormity* of his crime was appalling.
The *enormousness* of the Sahara exceeds that of any other desert.

enthused—should be avoided.
enthusiastic—is preferred.
Acceptable: We were *enthusiastic* over the performance.
Unacceptable: I am truly *enthused* about coming.

equally as good—is *unacceptable*.
just as good—is *acceptable*.
Acceptable: This book is *just as good* as that.
Unacceptable: Your marks are *equally as good* as mine.

everyone—is written as one word when it is a *pronoun*.

every one—(two words) is used when *each individual* is stressed.

Everyone present voted for the proposal.

Every one of the voters accepted the proposal.

NOTE: *Everybody* is written as one word.

every bit—is used colloquially for *just as*.

Acceptable: You are *just as* clever as she is.

Colloquial: He is *every bit* as lazy as his father.

everywheres—is *unacceptable*.

everywhere—is *acceptable*.

We searched *everywhere* for the missing book.

every which way—meaning *in all directions* is colloquial.

every way—is *acceptable*.

He tried to solve the problem *every way* he could.

exceed—means *going beyond the limit*.

excel—refers to *superior quality*.

You have *exceeded* the time allotted to you.

All-round athletes are expected to *excel* in many sports.

except—is *acceptable*.

excepting—is *unacceptable*.

Acceptable: All *except* Joe are going.
Unacceptable: All cities, *excepting* Washington, are in a state.
NOTE: Don't use *except* for *unless*.
He won't consent *unless* you give him the money.

exceptional—means *extraordinary*.
exceptionable—means *objectionable*.
Exceptional children learn to read before the age of five.
The behavior of exceptional children is sometimes *exceptionable*.

excessively—means *beyond acceptable limits*.
exceedingly—means *to a very great degree*.
In view of our recent feud, he was *excessively* friendly.
The weather in July was *exceedingly* hot.

expand—means *to spread out*.
expend—means *to use up*.
As the staff increases, we shall have to *expand* our office space.
Don't *expend* all your energy on one project.

factitious—means *unnatural* or *artificial*.
fictitious—means *imaginary*.
His *factitious* enthusiasm did not deceive us.
Jim Hawkins is a *fictitious* character.

faint—means *to lose consciousness*.
feint—means *to make a pretended attack*.
> The lack of fresh air caused her to *faint*.
> First he *feinted* to the left; then he lobbed the ball over the net.

farther—is used to describe *concrete distance*.
further—is used to describe *an extension of time or degree*.
> Chicago is *farther* from New York than is Cincinnati.
> I'll explain *further* my point of view.

feel bad—means to feel ill or sorry.
feel badly—is *unacceptable*.
> *Acceptable:* I *feel bad* about the accident I saw.
> *Unacceptable:* I *felt badly* when I saw her fall.

fever—refers to an *undue rise of temperature*.
temperature—refers to the *degree of heat* which may be normal.
> We had better call the doctor—he has a *fever*.
> The *temperature* is 80 degrees.

fewer—refers to *persons or things that can be counted*.
less—refers to *something considered as a mass*.
> We have *fewer* customers this week than last week.

I have *less* money in my pocket than you have.
But idiom: One *less* thing to worry about.

financial—refers to money matters in a *general sense*.

fiscal—refers to the *public treasury*.
Scholars are usually not *financial* successes.
The government's *fiscal year* begins July 1 and ends June 30.

flout—means *to show contempt for*.
flaunt—means *to make a display of*.
He *flouted* the authority of the principal.
She *flaunted* her wealth.

flowed—is the past participle of *flow*.
flown—is the past participle of *fly*.
The flood waters had *flowed* over the levee before nightfall.
He had *flown* for 500 hours before he crashed.

forbear—means *to refrain from doing something*.
forebear—means *ancestor*.
Forbear seeking vengeance.
Most of the family's *forebears* came from Ghana.

formally—means *in a formal way*.
formerly—means *at an earlier time*.

The letter of reference was *formally* written.
He was *formerly* a delegate to the convention.

former—means *the first of two*.
latter—means *the second of two*.
The *former* half of the book was prose.
The *latter* half of the book was poetry.

fort—means *a fortified place*.
forte—means *a strong point*.
A small garrison was able to hold the *fort*.
Conducting Wagner's music was Toscanini's
  forte.

forth—means *forward*.
fourth—*comes after third*.
They went *forth* like warriors of old.
The *Fourth* of July is our Independence Day.

freeze—means *to turn to ice*.
frieze—is *a decorated band in or on a building*.
As the temperature dropped, the water began to
  freeze.
The *friezes* on the Parthenon are wonders of art.

funny—means *humorous* or *laughable*.
That clown is truly *funny*.
Funny meaning *odd* or *strange* is a colloquial use.

genial—means *cheerful.*
congenial—means *agreeing in spirit.*
Genial landlords are rare today.
A successful party depends on *congenial* guests.

genius—means *extraordinary natural ability, or one so gifted.*
genus—means *class* or *kind.*
Mozart showed his *genius* for music at a very early age.
That flower probably does not belong to the *genus* of roses.

gibe / jibe—(pronounced alike)—both mean *to scoff.*
We are inclined to *gibe* at awkward speakers.
jibe also means *to agree.*
The two stories are now beginning to *jibe.*

got—means *obtained.* Colloquially, *got* has a sense of *obligation* or *possession.*
He *got* the tickets yesterday.
Not: We *have got* no sympathy for them.
But: We *have* no sympathy for them.
Colloquial: You've *got* to do it.
I've *got* two cats.

gourmand—is *one who eats large quantities of food.*
gourmet— (rhymes with poor-MAY) is *one who eats fastidiously; a connoisseur.*

His uncontrollable appetite soon turned him into a *gourmand*.

The *gourmet* chooses the right wine for each course.

graduated—is followed by *from*.

He *graduated* (or *was graduated*) *from* high school in 1997.

Unacceptable: He *graduated* college.

NOTE: A *graduated* test tube is one that has markings on it to indicate volume or capacity.

guess—is *colloquial* for *think* or *suppose*.

I *think* I'll go downtown.

habit—means an *individual* tendency to repeat a thing.

custom—means *group habit*.

He had a *habit* of breaking his glasses before each ball game.

The *custom* of the country was to eat fish raw.

had ought—is *unacceptable*.

You *ought* not to eat fish if you are allergic to it.

hanged—is used in reference to a *person*.

hung—is used in reference to a *thing*.

The prisoner was *hanged* at dawn.

The picture was *hung* above the fireplace.

healthy—means *having health.*
healthful—means *giving health.*
> The man is *healthy.*
> Fruit is *healthful.*

heap—means a *pile.*
heaps—is *slang* in the sense of *very much.*
> *Slang:* Thanks *heaps* for the gift.
> *Lots* is also *slang* for very much.

holy—means *sacred.*
holey—means *with holes.*
wholly—means *completely* or *altogether.*
> Easter Week is a *holy* time in many lands.
> Old socks tend to become *holey* after a while.
> We are *wholly* in agreement with your decision.

hypercritical—refers to a person *who finds fault easily.*
hypocritical—refers to a person *who pretends.*
> Don't be *hypercritical* about meals at low prices.
> It is better to be sincere than to be *hypocritical.*

idle—means *unemployed or unoccupied.*
idol—means *image* or *object of worship.*
> *Idle* men, like *idle* machines, are inclined to lose their sharpness.
> Some dictators prefer to be looked upon as *idols* by the masses.

immunity—implies *resistance to a disease*.
impunity—means *freedom from punishment*.
> The Salk vaccine helps develop an *immunity* to poliomyelitis.
> Because he was an only child, he frequently misbehaved with *impunity*.

imply—means *to suggest* or *hint at*. (The speaker *implies*.)
infer—means *to deduce* or *conclude*. (The listener *infers*.)
> Are you *implying* that I have disobeyed orders?
> From your carefree attitude, what else are we to *infer*?

inclement—(pronounced in-CLEM-ent) refers to *severe weather*, such as a heavy rainfall or storm. It does **not** mean threatening.
> Because of the *inclement* weather, we were soaked to the skin.

indict—(pronounced in-DITE) means *to charge with a crime*.
indite—means *to write*.
> The Grand Jury *indicted* him for embezzlement.
> Modern authors prefer the expression *to write*, rather than *indite;* the latter is now a stuffy sort of expression.

ingenious—means *skillful, imaginative.*
ingenuous—means *naive, frank,* or *candid.*
   The *ingenious* boy created his own rocket.
   One must be *ingenuous* to accept the Communist
      definition of freedom.

inside / inside of—When referring to time, use
   within.
   She is arriving *within* two hours.

irregardless—is *unacceptable.*
regardless—is *acceptable.*
   Not: *Irregardless* of the weather, I am going to
      the game.
   But: *Regardless* of his ability, he is not likely to
      win.

irresponsible—means *having no sense of responsibility.*
not responsible for—means *not accountable for
   something.*
   Irresponsible people are frequently late for
      appointments.
   Since you came late, we are *not responsible for*
      your having missed the first act.

its—means *belonging to it.*
it's—means *it is.*

The house lost *its* roof.
It's an exposed house, now.

join together—means to *unite* or *connect*. Omit the
redundant *together.*
Acceptable: I want to *join* these pieces of wood.
Unacceptable: All of us should *join together* to
fight intolerance.

judicial—means *pertaining to courts or to the law.*
judicious—means *wise.*
The problem required the *judicial* consideration
of an expert.
We were certainly in no position to make a
judicious decision.

kind of / sort of—are *colloquial* for *rather.*
What *kind of* car do you prefer?
We are *rather* disappointed in you.

last—refers to *the final member in a series.*
latest—refers to *the most recent in time.*
latter—refers to *the second of two.*
This is the *last* bulletin. (There won't be any other
bulletins.)
This is the *latest* bulletin. (There will be other
bulletins.)
Of the two most recent bulletins, the *latter* is more
encouraging.

later on—is *unacceptable* for *later*.
   Later, we shall give your request fuller attention.

least—means *the smallest*.
less—means *the smaller of two*.
   This was the *least* desirable of all the locations we have seen.
   We may finally have to accept the *less* desirable of the two locations we last saw.

leave—means *to go away from*.
let—means *to permit*.
   Leave this house at once.
   Let me remain in peace in my own house.

legible—means *able to be read*.
readable—means *able to be read with pleasure*.
   Your reports have become increasingly *legible*.
   In fact, I now find most of them extremely *readable*.

lengthened—means *made longer*.
lengthy—means *annoyingly long*.
   The essay, now *lengthened,* is more readable.
   However, try to avoid writing *lengthy* explanations of obvious facts.

levy—means *to impose a tax*.
levee—means *an embankment*.

It is the duty of Congress to *levy* taxes.

The Mississippi River is contained by massive *levees*.

libel—is *a written and published statement injurious to a person's character.*

slander—is *a spoken statement of the same sort.*

The unfavorable references to me in your book are *libel*.

When you say these vicious things about me, you are committing *slander*.

lightening—is the present participle of *to lighten.*

lightning—means *the flashes of light accompanied by thunder.*

Lightening the pack made it easier to carry.

Summer thunderstorms produce startling *lightning* bolts.

line—meaning *occupation* is *unacceptable.*

Acceptable: He is in the engineering *profession.*

Unacceptable: What *line* are you in?

lineament—means *outline* or *contour.*

liniment—is a *medicated liquid.*

His face had the *lineaments* of a Greek Adonis.

After the football games, we all applied *liniment* to our legs.

loan—is a *noun*.
lend—is a *verb*.
The bank was willing to grant him a *loan* of $500.
The bank was willing to *lend* him $500.

lonely—means *longing for companionship*.
solitary—means *isolated*.
Some people are forced to live *lonely* lives.
Sometimes *solitary* surroundings are conducive
to deep thought.

luxuriant—means *abundant growth*.
luxurious—implies *wealth*.
One expects to see *luxuriant* plants in the tropics.
The *luxurious* surroundings indicated both wealth
and good taste.

majority—means *more than half of the total
number.*
plurality—means *an excess of votes received by the
leading candidate over those received by the next
candidate.*

Example:	A	received	251	votes.
	B	received	127	votes.
	C	received	123	votes.

A received a *majority,* or one vote more than half
of the total.
A received a *plurality* of 124 votes over B.

many—refers to *a number*.

much—refers to *a quantity in bulk*.

> How *many* inches of rain fell last night?
>
> I don't know, but I would say *much* rain fell last night.

material—means *of or pertaining to matter*.

materiel—(accent the last syllable) is French, and means *material equipment,* the opposite of *personnel* (*manpower*).

> His *material* assets included an automobile and two suits of clothing.
>
> The small army was rich in *materiel,* poor in personnel.

may—is used in the *present tense*.

might—is used in the *past tense*.

> We are hoping that he *may* come today.
>
> He *might* have done it if you had encouraged him.

it's I—is always *acceptable*.

it's me—is *acceptable* in informal speech or writing.

It's he / This is she / It was they—are always *acceptable*.

It's him / This is her / It was them—are informal.

measles—is plural in form, singular in meaning.
Measles is now a minor childhood disease.
NOTE: *Mumps* and *shingles* are also singular in meaning.

medieval—means of or pertaining to *the Middle Ages*.
middle-aged—refers to persons *in the middle period of life*.
Serfs and feudal baronies were part of *medieval* times.
According to the Bible, the *middle-aged* man has thirty-five more years of life to look forward to.

Messrs.—(rhymes with *guessers*) is the plural of *Mr. Misters* is *unacceptable*.
The meeting was attended by *Messrs.* Smith, Jones, Brown, and Swift.

metal—is a type of *substance*.
mettle—means *spirit*.
Lead is one of the more familiar *metals*.
One had to admire his *mettle* in the face of a crisis.

minutiae—(pronounced min-EW-she-ee) is the plural of *minutia,* and means *minor details*.
A meticulous person spends much time on *minutiae*.

Mmes.—(pronounced me-DAM) is the abbreviation for *Mesdames,* the plural of *Madam.* It introduces a series of names of married women.

> The party was attended by the *Mmes.* Jones, Smith, and Wilson.

> The plural of *Miss* is *Misses.*

moneys—is *the plural of money.* (also monies)

> We shall vote on the disposition of the various *moneys* in the treasury.

moral—means *good or ethical;* also, an *ethical lesson to be drawn.*

morale—(pronounced more-AL) means *spirit.*

> The *moral* of the story is that it pays to be honest.

> The *morale* of the troops rose after the general's inspiring speech.

most—is an adverb in the *superlative degree.*

almost—is an adverb meaning *nearly.*

> He is the *most* courteous boy in the class.

> It's *almost* time to go to school.

nauseous—means *causing sickness.*

nauseated—means *being sick.*

> The odor is *nauseous.*

> I feel *nauseated.*

naval—refers to *ships*.
nautical—refers to *navigation and seamen*.
  John Paul Jones was a famous *naval* commander.
  A *nautical* mile is a little longer than a land mile.

neither—means *not either of two,* and should **not**
  be used for *none* or *not one*.
  Neither of his two books was very popular.
  Of the many plays he has written, *not one* (or
    none) was good.

noplace—is *unacceptable* for *no place* or *nowhere*.
  You now have *nowhere* to go.

nohow—is *unacceptable for regardless*.
  Unacceptable: I can't do this nohow.

notable—means *remarkable*.
notorious—means *of bad reputation*.
  December 7, 1941, was a *notable* day.
  At that time, the *notorious* Tojo commanded the
    Japanese forces.

nothing more or less—is *unacceptable* for *nothing
  more nor less*.
  Using correct English is *nothing more nor less*
    than a matter of careful practice.

nowhere near—is *unacceptable* for *not nearly*.
  The work was *not nearly* finished by nightfall.

nowheres—is *unacceptable*.
nowhere—is *acceptable*.
  The child was *nowhere* to be found.

number—is singular *when the total is intended*.
number—is plural when the individual units are
  referred to.
  The *number* of pages in the book is 500.
  A *number* of pages were printed in italic type.

obligate—implies a *moral or legal responsibility*.
oblige—means *to do as a favor* or *to accommodate*.
  The principal felt *obligated* to disqualify himself
    in the dispute between the pupils.
  Please *oblige* me by refraining from discussing
    this matter with anyone else.

observance—means the *act of complying*.
observation—means the *act of noting*.
  In *observance* of the new regulation, we shall omit
    further tests.
  His scientific *observations* became the basis for
    a new rocket theory.

occupancy—refers to *the mere act of occupying,*
  usually legally.

occupation—means *the forceful act of occupying*.
According to the lease, the tenant still had
occupancy of the apartment for another month.
The *occupation* of the town by troops worried
the townspeople.

oculist or ophthalmologist—is an MD who *treats
diseases of the eye*.
optometrist—is a person who *measures the eye* to
prescribe glasses.
optician—is a person who *makes the glasses*.
An *oculist* is also called an *ophthalmologist*.
An *optometrist* may also be an *optician*.

of any—(and *of anyone*) is *unacceptable* for *of all*.
His was the highest mark *of all*.

off of—is *unacceptable*. Omit *of*.
He took the book *off* the table.

OK—(or *okay*) is used for *acceptable* or *approved*
in informal business and informal social usage.
Avoid the use of OK in formal situations.

on account of—is *unacceptable* for *because*.
We could not meet you *because* we did not receive your message in time.

oral—means *spoken*.

verbal—means *expressed in words,* either spoken or written.

> In international intrigue, *oral* messages are less risky than written ones.

> Shorthand must usually be transcribed into *verbal* form.

ordinance—means *regulation*.

ordnance—refers to *guns, cannon, and the like.*

> The local *ordinance* restricted driving speeds to 35 miles an hour.

> Some rockets and guided missiles are now included in military *ordnance*.

ostensible—means *shown* (usually for the purpose of deceiving others).

ostentatious—means *showy*.

> Although he was known to be ambitious, his *ostensible* motive was civic pride.

> His *ostentatious* efforts in behalf of civic improvement impressed no one.

other . . . than—is acceptable; other . . . but (or other . . . except) is unacceptable.

> We have no *other* motive *than* friendship.

other—is an adjective and means *different*.

otherwise—is an adverb and means *in a different way*.

What you did was *other* than what you had
  promised.

I cannot look *otherwise* than with delight at the
  improvement in your work.

out loud—is *colloquial* for *aloud.*

He read *aloud* to his family every evening.

outdoor—is an adjective.

outdoors—is an adverb.

We spent most of the summer at an *outdoor*
  music camp.

Most of the time we played string quartets *out-*
  doors.

Out-of-doors is *acceptable* in either case.

part from—*a person.*

part with—*a thing.*

It was difficult for her to *part from* her classmates.

It will be difficult for him to *part with* his car.

party—refers to a *group,* **not** an *individual.*

person—refers to an *individual.*

A *party* of men went on a scouting mission.

Who is the *person* you came with?

NOTE: *Party* may be used for the word *person* in
  a legal document.

pedal—means *a lever operated by foot.* (avoid foot pedal)

peddle—means *to sell from door to door.*

It is impossible to ride a bicycle without moving the *pedals*.

The traveling salesman *peddling* brushes is a thing of the past.

percent—(also **per cent**) expresses *rate of interest.*

percentage—means *a part or proportion of the whole.*

The interest rate of some banks is 4 *percent*.

The census showed the *percentage* of unmarried people to have increased.

persecute—means *to make life miserable for someone.*

prosecute—means *to conduct a criminal investigation.*

Some racial groups insist upon *persecuting* other groups.

The District Attorney is *prosecuting* the racketeers.

personal—refers to *a person.*

personnel—means *an organized body of individuals.*

The general took a *personal* interest in every one of his men.

He believed that this was necessary in order to maintain the morale of the *personnel* in his division.

physic—means *a drug*.
physics—is *a branch of science*.
physique—means *body structure*.
   A doctor should determine the safe dose of a *physic*.
   Nuclear *physics* is one of the most challenging of the sciences.
   Athletes must take care of their *physiques*.

plenty—is a noun; it means *abundance*.
   America is a land of *plenty*.
   There is *plenty of* (**not** *plenty*) room in the compact car for me.
   Plenty as an adverb is *colloquial*.
   The compact car is *quite* large enough for me.

pole—means a long stick.
poll—means *vote*.
   We bought a new *pole* for the flag.
   The seniors took a *poll* to determine the graduate most likely to succeed.

poorly—meaning *in poor health* is *unacceptable in formal usage*.

Grandfather was feeling *in poor health* all last
winter.

pour—is *to send flowing with direction and control.*
spill—is *to send flowing accidentally.*
　Please *pour* some cream into my cup of coffee.
　Careless people *spill* things.

practicable—means *usable* or *workable* and is
　applied only to objects.
practical—means *realistic, having to do with
　action.* It applies to persons and things.
　There is as yet no *practicable* method for resist-
　ing atomic bomb attacks.
　Practical technicians, nevertheless, are attempt-
　ing to translate the theories of the atomic
　scientists into some form of defense.

precede—means *to come before.*
proceed—means *to go ahead.* (*procedure* is the
　noun)
supersede—means *to replace.*
　What are the circumstances that *preceded* the
　attack?
　We can then *proceed* with our plan for resisting a
　second attack.
　It is then possible that Plan B will *supersede*
　Plan A.

prescribe—means *to lay down a course of action*.

proscribe—means *to outlaw* or *forbid*.

> The doctor *prescribed* plenty of rest and good food for the man.
>
> Some towns may *proscribe* various forms of expression.

principal—means *chief* or *main* (as an adjective); *a leader* (as a noun).

principle—means *a fundamental truth* or *belief*.

> His *principal* supporters came from among the peasants.
>
> The *principal* of the school asked for cooperation from the staff.
>
> Humility was the guiding *principle* of Buddha's life.
>
> NOTE: *principal* may also mean a sum placed at interest.
>
> Part of his monthly payment was applied as interest on the *principal*.

prodigy—means a *person endowed with extraordinary gifts or powers*.

protégé—means *someone under the protection of another*.

> Mozart was a musical *prodigy* at the age of three.
>
> For a time, Schumann was the *protégé* of Johannes Brahms.

prophecy—(rhymes with *sea*) is the noun meaning *prediction.*

prophesy—(rhymes with *sigh*) is a verb meaning *to predict.*

The *prophecy* of the three witches eventually misled Macbeth.

The witches had *prophesied* that Macbeth would become king.

put in—meaning *to spend, make,* or *devote* is *colloquial.*

Every good student should *spend* (or *put in*) at least four hours a day in studying.

Be sure to *make* (or *put in*) an appearance at the council meeting.

rain—means *water from the clouds.*

reign—means *rule.*

rein—means *a strap for guiding a horse.*

The *rain* in Spain falls mainly on the plain.

A queen now *reigns* over England.

When the *reins* were pulled too tightly, the horse reared.

real—meaning *very* or *extremely* is *colloquial.*

He is a *very* handsome young man.

He is *really* handsome.

reason is because—is *unacceptable* for *reason is that.*

    The *reason* young people do not read Trollope today *is that* his sentences are too involved.

    Avoid *due to* after *reason is.*

    The *reason* he refused *was that* he was proud (**not** *due to* his pride).

rebellion—means *open, armed, or organized resistance to authority.*

revolt—means *similar resistance on a smaller scale.*

revolution—means *the overthrowing of one government and the setting up of another.*

    Bootlegging has sometimes been referred to as a *rebellion* against high whiskey taxes.

    An increase in the grain tax caused a peasants' *revolt* against the landowners.

    Unpopular regimes are often overthrown in violent *revolutions.*

reckon—meaning *suppose* or *think* is *unacceptable.*

    I *think* it may rain this afternoon.

recollect—means *to bring back to memory.*

remember—means *to keep in memory.*

    Now I can *recollect* your returning the money to me.

    I *remember* the occasion well.

reconcile to—means *resign to* or *adjust to*.

reconcile with—means *to become friendly again with someone;* also, *to bring one set of facts into harmony with another one*.

I am now *reconciled to* this chronic ache in my back.

George was *reconciled with* his parents after many years.

How does one *reconcile* the politician's shabby accomplishments *with* the same politician's noble promises?

regular—meaning *real* or *true* is *colloquial*.
Colloquial: He was a *regular* tyrant.
Preferred: He was a *true* tyrant.

respectably—means *in a manner deserving respect*.
respectfully—means *with respect and decency*.
respectively—means *as relating to each, in the order given*.

Young people should conduct themselves *respectably* in school as well as in church.

The students listened *respectfully* to the principal.

John and Bill are the sons *respectively* of Mr. Smith and Mr. Brown.

reverend—means *worthy of reverence or respect*.
reverent—means *feeling or showing respect*.

Shakespeare, the *reverend* master of the drama, still inspires most readers.

Sometimes a too *reverent* attitude toward Shakespeare causes the reader to miss much of the fun in his plays.

rob—One *robs a person or institution.*
steal—One *steals a thing.*
  They *robbed* the man of his money.
  He *stole* my wallet.

rout—(rhymes with *stout*) means *a defeat.*
route—(rhymes with either *boot* or *stout*) means *a way of travel.*
  The *rout* of the army was near.
  The salesman has a steady *route.*

same as—is *colloquial* for *in the same way as* and *just as.*
  The owner's son was treated *in the same way as* any other worker.
  Avoid *same* as a pronoun, except in *legal* usage.
  If the books are available, please send *them* (**not** *same*) by parcel post.

self-confessed—is *redundant* for *confessed.* Omit *self.*
  He was a *confessed* lover of chocolate.

sensible of—means *aware of.*
sensitive to—means *affected by.*
    I am very *sensible of* my shortcomings.
    He is *sensitive to* criticism.

shape—meaning *condition* is *colloquial.*
    The refugees were in a serious *condition* (or *shape*) when they arrived here.

show up—meaning *to expose* is *unacceptable.*
    It is my firm intention to *expose* (**not** *show up*) your hypocrisy.

simple reason—is *unacceptable* for *reason.* Omit the word *simple* in similar expressions: *simple truth, simple purpose,* etc.
    Unacceptable: I refuse to do it for the *simple reason* that I don't like your attitude.
    Acceptable: The *truth* is that I feel tired.

simply—meaning *absolutely* or *extremely* is often redundant.
    Not: The performance was *simply* thrilling.
    But: The performance was thrilling.

size up—meaning *to estimate* is *colloquial.*
    The detectives were able *to estimate* (or *size up*) the fugitive's remaining ammunition supply.

sociable—means *friendly.*
social—means *relating to people in general.*
> *Sociable* individuals prefer to have plenty of people around them.
> The President's *social* program was just another waste.

sole—means *all alone.*
soul—means *human spirit.*
> He was the *sole* owner of the business.
> Man's *soul* is unconquerable.

some time—means *a portion of time.*
sometime—means *at an indefinite time in the future.*
sometimes—means *occasionally.*
> I'll need *some time* to make a decision.
> Let us meet *sometime* after noon.
> *Sometimes* it is better to hesitate before signing a contract.

somewheres—is *unacceptable.*
somewhere—is *acceptable.*

specie—means *money as coins.* (*Specie* is singular only.)
species—means *a member of a group of related things.* (*Species* is singular and plural.)

He preferred to be paid in *specie,* rather than in
  bank notes.
The human *species* is relatively young. (singular)
Many animal *species* existed before man.
  (plural)

stand—meaning *to tolerate* is *colloquial.*
  I refuse *to tolerate* (or *to stand for*) crime.

state—means *to declare formally.*
say—means *to speak.*
  Our ambassador *stated* the terms for a ceasefire.
  We *said* that we would not attend the meeting.

stationary—means *standing still.*
stationery—means *writing materials.*
  In ancient times people thought the earth was
    stationary.
  We bought writing paper at the *stationery* store.

statue—means *a piece of sculpture.*
statute—is *a law.*
  The *Statue* of Liberty stands in New York Harbor.
  Compulsory education was established by *statute.*

summons—is singular; *summonses* is the plural.
  We received a *summons* to appear in court.
  This was the first of three *summonses* we were to
    receive that week.

surround—means *to enclose on all sides*. Do **not** add *on all sides* to it.

The camp was *surrounded* by heavy woods.

take in—is *colloquial* in the sense of *deceive* or *attend*.

We were *deceived* (or *taken in*) by her charming manner.

We should like to *attend* (or *take in*) a few plays during our vacation.

tasteful—means *having good taste*.
tasty—means *pleasing to the taste*.

The home of our host was decorated in a *tasteful* manner.

Our host also served us very *tasty* meals.

tenants—are *occupants*.
tenets—are *principles*.

Several *tenants* occupied that apartment during the first month.

His religious *tenets* led him to perform many good deeds.

tender—means *to offer officially or formally*.
give—means *to donate* or *surrender something willingly*.

The discredited official decided to *tender* his resignation.

He *gave* testimony readily before the grand jury.

testimony—means *information given orally only*.
evidence—means *information given orally or in writing*.

He gave *testimony* to the grand jury.

The defendant presented written *evidence* to prove he was not at the scene of the crime.

that there / this here—are *unacceptable*. Omit *there, here*.

That person is taller than *this* one.

their—means *belonging to them*.
there—means *in that place*.
they're—means *they are*.

We took *their* books home with us.

You will find your books over *there* on the desk.

They're not as young as we expected them to be.

theirselves—is *unacceptable* for *themselves*.

Most children of school age are able to care for *themselves* in many ways.

therefor—means *for that*.
therefore—means *because of that*.

One day's detention is the punishment *therefor.*
You will, *therefore*, have to remain in school
after dismissal time.

these kind—is *unacceptable.*
this kind—is *acceptable.*
I am fond of *this kind* of apples.
(*These kinds* would also be *acceptable.*)

tortuous—means *twisting.*
torturing—means *causing pain.*
The wagon train followed a *tortuous* trail through
the mountains.
The *torturing* memory of his defeat kept him
awake all night.

track—means *a path* or *road.*
tract—means *a brief but serious piece of writing* or
a piece of land.
The horses raced around the *track.*
John Locke wrote a famous *tract* on education.
The heavily wooded *tract* was sold to a lumber
company.

ulterior—means *lying beyond or hidden underneath.*
underlying—means *fundamental.*
His noble words were contradicted by his
ulterior motives.

Shakespeare's *underlying* motive in *Hamlet* was
to criticize the moral climate of his own times.

unique—means *the only one of its kind,* and therefore
does not take *very, most,* or *extremely* before it.
The First Folio edition of Shakespeare's works is
unique (**not** *very unique*).
NOTE: The same rule applies to *perfect.*

upwards of—is *colloquial* for *more than.*
There are *more than* (or *upwards of*) one million
people living in Idaho today.

valuable—means *of great worth.*
valued—means *held in high regard.*
invaluable—means *priceless.*
This is a *valuable* manuscript.
The expert gave him highly *valued* advice.
A good name is an *invaluable* possession.

venal—means *corrupted.*
The *venal* councilwoman accepted the bribe.

veracity—means *truthfulness.*
truth—is *a true statement, a fact.*
Because he had a reputation for *veracity,* we could
not doubt his story.
We would have questioned the *truth* of his story
otherwise.

via—means *by way of* and should be used in connection with travel or motion only.

We shipped the merchandise *via* motor express.

I received the information *through* (**not** *via*) his letter.

virtue—means *goodness*.

virtuosity—means *technical skill*.

We should expect a considerable degree of *virtue* in our public officials.

The young pianist played with amazing *virtuosity* at his debut.

virtually—means *in effect*.

actually—means *in fact*.

A tie in the final game was *virtually* a defeat for us.

We had *actually* won more games than they.

waive—means *to give up*.

wave—means *a swell* or *roll of water*.

As a citizen, I refuse to *waive* my right of free speech.

The *waves* reached the top deck of the ship.

whereabouts—is *colloquial* for *where* but only as a noun meaning *location*.

Not: *Whereabouts* do you live?

But: Do you know his *whereabouts?*

whose—means *of whom.*
who's—means *who is.*
> *Whose* is this notebook?
> *Who's* in the next office?

would have—is unacceptable for *had.*
> I wish you *had* (**not** *would have*) called earlier.

ABBREVIATIONS

Established abbreviations are acceptable in all but the most formal writing. For reading ease, use only well-known abbreviations. If it is desirable to use an abbreviation that may not be familiar to the reader, spell out the word or phrase in parentheses after the abbreviation the first time you use it. After this first definition, the abbreviation may be used without further explanation. Abbreviations should be consistent throughout a text.

PUNCTUATION

1. In general, an abbreviation follows the capitalization and hyphenation of the original word or phrase. Each element may or may not be followed by a period. The current trend is to omit the periods where they used to be required. Note, however, that abbreviations of courtesy titles, initials, addresses, business names, calendar dates, and Latin terms generally retain their periods.

USMC	KGB
AFL-CIO	NATO
NT (New Testament)	SW (in an address following a street name)

2. Periods are omitted from abbreviations of units of measure in scientific or technical writing:

km	cm^3
ft-lb	g
dB	FM

In non-technical writing, abbreviated units of English measure may be typed with or without periods. Use a period if leaving it out would create confusion.

3. Abbreviations with periods should be typed without spaces, except for initials in personal names:

A.D.	etc.
T. S. Eliot	R. S. Baker, MD

The initials of American presidents, however, are typed without spaces or periods:

JFK	RMN	WJC

GEOGRAPHIC TERMS

1. You may abbreviate *United States* when preceding *Government* or the name of a Government organization, except in formal writing. Spell out *United States* when it is used as a noun or when it is used as an adjective in association with names of other countries.

   > US Government

   > US Congress

   > US Department of Agriculture

   > US monitor *Nantucket*

   > USS *Brooklyn* (note abbreviation for ship)

   > *but* The position taken by the United States,

   > British, and French governments.

2. With the exceptions just noted, the abbreviation US is used in the adjective position, but is spelled out when used as a noun.

US foreign policy	*but* foreign policy of the United States
US economy	the economy of the United States

US attorney	United States Code (official title)
US troops	United States Steel Corp. (legal title)

3. Words in an address are usually spelled out. Where brevity is required, the following abbreviations may be used. Note that compass directions do not use periods.

St.—Street	Dr.—Drive
Ave.—Avenue	Ct.—Court
Pl.—Place	Bldg.—Building
Sq.—Square	NW—Northwest
Blvd.—Boulevard	SW—Southwest
Terr.—Terrace	NE—Northeast
SE—Southeast	

4. Spell out the names of the US states and territories when they are used alone or follow another name (such as that of a city) in ordinary text. If space is limited, as in tabular work, use the abbreviations given on the left. Use the official two-letter postal abbreviations with zip code for anything being mailed.

Ala.	AL	La.	LA
Alaska	AK	Maine	ME
Ariz.	AZ	Md.	MD
Ark.	AR	Mass.	MA
Calif.	CA	Mich.	MI
Colo.	CO	Minn.	MN
Conn.	CT	Miss.	MS
Del.	DE	Mo.	MO
DC	DC	Mont.	MT
Fla.	FL	Nebr.	NE
Ga.	GA	Nev.	NV
Guam	GU	NH	NH
Hawaii	HI	NJ	NJ
Idaho.	ID	N. Mex.	NM
Ill.	IL	NY	NY
Ind.	IN	NC	NC
Iowa	IA	N. Dak.	ND
Kans.	KS	Ohio	OH
Ky.	KY	Okla.	OK

Ore.	OR	Utah	UT
Pa	PA	Vt.	VT
PR	PR (Puerto Rico)	Va.	VA
RI	RI	VI	VI (Virgin Islands)
Amer. Samoa	AS	Wash.	WA
		W.Va.	WV
SC	SC	Wis. (or Wisc.)	WI
S. Dak.	SD		
Tenn.	TN	Wyo.	WY
Tex.	TX		

The names of countries are usually not abbreviated.

NAMES AND TITLES

1. Use abbreviations in company names as they are shown on the company's letterhead.

   J. Dillard & Sons, Inc.

2. Where brevity in company names is required, the following abbreviations may be used:

Bros.—Brothers   Inc.—Incorporated

Co.—Company   Ltd.—Limited

Corp.—Corporation   &—and

Do not abbreviate *Company* and *Corporation* in names of Federal Government units.

Metals Reserve Company

Commodity Credit Corporation

3. In other than formal usage, you may abbreviate a civil or a military title preceding a name if followed by the person's given name or initial as well as the surname.

Adj.—Adjutant

Adm. (or ADM)—Admiral

Asst. Surg.—Assistant Surgeon

Brig. Gen.—Brigadier General

Capt.—Captain

Col.—Colonel

Comdr.—Commander

Cpl.—Corporal

CWO—Chief Warrant Officer

1st Lt.—First Lieutenant

1st Sgt.—First Sergeant

Gen.—General

Gov.—Governor

Lt. (or Lieut.)—Lieutenant

Lt. Comdr.—Lieutenant Commander

LTC (or Lt. Col.)—Lieutenant Colonel

LTG (or Lt. Gen.)—Lieutenant General

LTJG—Lieutenant, junior grade)

Maj.—Major

Maj. Gen.—Major General

M. Sgt.—Master Sergeant

Pfc. (or PFC)—Private, first class

PO—Petty Officer

Prof.—Professor

Pvt.—Private

Rear Adm.—Rear Admiral

2d Lt.—Second Lieutenant

Sfc.—Sergeant, first class

Sgt.—Sergeant

SGM (or Sgt. Maj)—Sergeant Major

S. Sgt.—Staff Sergeant

Supt.—Superintendent

Surg.—Surgeon

TSgt.—Technical Sergeant

Vice Adm.—Vice Admiral

WO—Warrant Officer

4. Use the following abbreviations after a name:

Jr., Sr.

2d, 3d, II, III (not preceded by a comma)

5. Fellowships, orders, etc.:

BPOE (Benevolent and Protective Order of Elks),

KCB (Knight Commander of the Order of Bath)

6. *Sr.* and *Jr.* should be used with the full given name and initials, and in combination with any title.

Anthony Baxter Jones, Jr.; *or* A. B. Jones, Sr.

7. Do not use titles such as *Mr., Mrs., Ms., Dr.,* or *Esq.* in combination with another title or with abbreviations indicating academic degrees.

> John Jones, MA, PhD; *not* Mr. John Jones, MA, PhD

> David Roe, MD; *not* Dr. David Roe, MD, *nor* Mr. David Roe, MD

> Gerald West, Esq. *not* Mr. Gerald West, Esq., *nor* Gerald West, Esq., PhD

8. Although academic degrees are abbreviations of Latin terms, the punctuation and, in some cases, the spacing are often omitted.

> MA, PhD, LLD

9. When a name is followed by abbreviations designating religious and fraternal orders and academic and honorary degrees, arrange the abbreviations in this sequence: Orders, religious first; theological degrees; academic degrees earned in course; and honorary degrees in order of bestowal.

> John J. Jones, DD, MA, DLit

> Richard R. Row, CSC, PhD, LLD

PARTS OF PUBLICATIONS

Abbreviations may be used to designate parts of publications mentioned in parentheses, brackets, footnotes, lists of references, and tables, and followed by figures, letters, or Roman numerals. Note that these abbreviations retain their periods.

App., apps.,—appendix, appendixes

art., arts.—article, articles

bull., bulls.—bulletin, bulletins

cl., cls.—clause, clauses

chap., chaps.—chapter, chapters

col., cols.—column, columns

fig., figs.—figure, figures

no., nos.—number, numbers

p., pp.—page, pages

par., pars.—paragraph, paragraphs

pl., pls.—plate, plates

pt., pts.—part, parts

sec., secs.—section, sections

subchap., subchaps.—subchapter, subchapters

subpar., subpars.—subparagraph, sub-
paragraphs

subsec., subsecs.—subsection, subsections

supp., supps.—supplement, supplements

vol., vols.—volume, volumes

CALENDAR DIVISIONS

When brevity is required, you may abbreviate the names of months—except May, June and July— when used with day, or year, or both.

Jan. Feb. Mar. Apr. Aug. Sept. (or Sep.) Oct. Nov. Dec.

Similarly the names of days of the week may be abbreviated.

Sun. Mon. Tues. Wed. Thurs. Fri. Sat.

STANDARD WORD ABBREVIATIONS

AA or **A.A.,** Alcoholics Annonymous, antiaircraft, Associate in Arts, Administration on Aging
AAA, American Automobile Association, antiaircraft artillery

AB or **A.B.** or **BA** or **B.A.,** bachelor of arts

abbr. or **abbrev.,** abbreviated or abbreviation

ABC, American Bowling Congress; American Broadcasting Company; atomic, biological, and chemical

abs., absolute, abstract

AC or **A.C.,** alternating current, Athletic Club

A/C, air conditioning

acct., account, accountant

ACDA, Arms Control and Disarmament Agency

ACTH, adrenocorticotropic hormone

ACTION, not an acronym, but an independent Federal agency

AD or **A.D.,** active duty; Anno Domini, in the year of our Lord

ADP, automatic data processing

AEC, Atomic Energy Commission

AEF, American Expeditionary Force (or Forces)

AFB, Air Force Base

AFL-CIO, American Federation of Labor and Congress of Industrial Organizations

AID, Agency for International Development

aka, also known as

ALR, American Law Reports

AM or **A.M.,** *ante meridiem,* before noon; master of arts (see also **MA** or **M.A.**)

AMC, American Maritime Cases

Am Dec, American Decisions

AMG, Allied Military Government

Am Repts, American Reports
AMVETS, American Veterans of World War II, Amvet(s) (individual)
antilog, antilogarithm
API, American Petroleum Institute
APO, Army and Air Force Post Office (overseas)
App DC, District of Columbia Appeal Cases
App Div, Appellate Division
APPR, Army Package Power Reactor
approx., approximate, approximately
ARC, American Red Cross, AIDS-related complex
ARPA, Advanced Research Projects Agency
ARS, Agricultural Research Service
ASCS, Agricultural Stabilization and Conservation Service
ASME, American Society of Mechanical Engineers
ASN, Army Service Number
Asst. Surg., assistant surgeon
AST, Atlantic Standard Time
ASTM, American Society for Testing and Materials
AT, Atlantic Time
Atl, Atlantic; Atlantic Reporter; **A.(2d),** Atlantic Reporter, second series
AUS, Austria, Army of the United States
AWL, Absent With Leave
AWOL, Absent Without Official Leave
BAE, Bureau of Agricultural Economics
BCG, (bacillus Calmette-Guerin), anti-tuberculosis vaccine

BDSA, Business and Defense Services Administration
Bé, Baumé
BEC, Bureau of Employees' Compensation
bf, boldface
BIA, Bureau of Indian Affairs
BIS, Bank for International Settlements
Blatch Pr Cas, Blatchford's Prize Cases
bldg., building
BLit(t) or **B.Lit(t)** or **Lit(t)B** or **Lit(t).B.,** Bachelor of Letters (or Literature)
BLM, Bureau of Land Management
BLS, Bachelor of Library Science, Bureau of Labor Statistics
BNDD, Bureau of Narcotics and Dangerous Drugs
bo, back order, bad order, buyer's option
BS or **B.S.,** Bachelor of Science
CAB, Civil Aeronautics Board
CACM, Central American Common Market
c. and sc., caps and small caps
CAP, Civil Air Patrol
CARE, Cooperative for American Relief Everywhere, Inc
cbd, cash before delivery
CCA, Circuit Court of Appeals
CCC, Civilian Conservation Corps, Commodity Credit Corporation
CCls, Court of Claims
CClsR, Court of Claims Reports
CCPA, Court of Customs and Patent Appeals

CCR, Commission on Civil Rights

CE, Christian (or Common) Era

CEA, Council of Economic Advisers, Commodity Exchange Authority

CEC, Commodity Exchange Commission

Cento., Central Treaty Organization

CFR, Code of Federal Regulations

CFR Suppl., Code of Federal Regulations Supplement

CIA, Central Intelligence Agency

CIC, Counterintelligence Corps

CJ, *corpus juris,* body of law; Chief Justice

CMS, Consumer Marketing Service

CO, Commanding Officer

COD or **cod,** cash (or collect) on delivery

col., collateral, collected, collector, college, colony, color, column

COL, cost of living

Comp. Dec., Comptroller's Decisions (Treasury)

Comp. Gen. Dec., Comptroller General Decisions

con., consolidated, consul, continued

CONELRAD, control of electromagnetic radiation (civil defense)

cos, cash on shipment, companies, cosine, counties

cosh, hyperbolic cosine

cot, cotangent

coth, hyperbolic cotangent

cp, candlepower, chemically pure, compare

CPA, Certified Public Accountant

CPI, Consumer Price Index
CPR, cardiopulmonary resuscitation
cr, credit, creditor
CRP, C-reactive protein
CSC, Civil Service Commission
csc, cosecant
csch, hyperbolic cosecant
CSS, Commodity Stabilization Service
CST, Central Standard Time
ct or **ct.,** cent, county, court
CT, Central Time
CWO, cash with order (cwo), Chief Warrant Officer
Dall, Dallas (U.S. Supreme Court Reports)
DAR, Daughters of the American Revolution
DATA, Defense Air Transportation Administration
dba, doing business as
dbh, diameter at breast height
DC, direct current, District of Columbia
DD or **D.D.,** Doctor of Divinity
DDS or **D.D.S.,** Doctor of Dental Surgery
DDT, dichlorodiphenyltrichloroethane
DEW, distant early warning (DEW line)
Dist. Ct., District Court
DLF, Development Loan Fund
Dlit(t) or **D.Lit(t)** or **Lit(t)D** or **Lit(t).D.,** Doctor of
  Literature
DMB, Defense Mobilization Board
DOD, Department of Defense
DOT, Department of Transportation

DP, dew point, displaced person, double play
DPH, Doctor of Public Health
DPHy, Doctor of Public Hygiene
dr, debit, debtor, drachma, dram
DSA, Defense Supply Agency
DV, distinguished visitor (Air Force) (see also **VIP**)
DVM, Doctor of Veterinary Medicine
Ecosoc, Economic and Social Council
EDT, Eastern Daylight Time
EEC, European Economic Community
EEE, Eastern Equine Encephalitis
EFTA, European Free Trade Association
EHS, Environmental Health Services
8°, octavo
emcee, master of ceremony
eom, end of month
EOP, Executive Office of the President
EPA, Environmental Protection Agency
ERP, European Recovery Program
ESSA, Environmental Science Services Administration
EST, Eastern Standard Time
ET, Eastern Time
Euratom, European Atomic Energy Community
Euromarket, European Common Market (European
   Economic Community)
Euromart, see Euromarket
Ex. Doc., executive document
FAA, Federal Aviation Administration
FAO, Food and Agriculture Organization

fas, free alongside ship
FAS, Foreign Agricultural Service
FBI, Federal Bureau of Investigation
FCA, Farm Credit Administration
FCC, Federal Communications Commission
FCIC, Federal Crop Insurance Corporation
FCSC, Foreign Claims Settlement Commission
FDA, Food and Drug Administration
FDIC, Federal Deposit Insurance Corporation
FDL, fast deployment logistic (ship)
Fed, Federal, Federation
FHA, Federal Housing Administration, Farmers
　　Home Administration
FHLBB, Federal Home Loan Bank Board
FICA, Federal Insurance Contributions Act
FLSA, Fair Labor Standards Act
FM, frequency modulation
FMC, Federal Maritime Commission
FMCS, Federal Mediation and Conciliation Service
FNMA, Federal National Mortgage Association
　　(Fannie May)
FNS, Food and Nutrition Service
FOB or **fob,** free on board
FPC, Federal Power Commission
FPIS, forward propagation ionospheric scatter
FPO, Fleet Post Office
FPV, free piston vessel
FR, Federal Register (publication)

FRS, Fellow of the Royal Society, Federal Reserve System

FS, Forest Service

FSA, Federal Security Agency

FSS, Federal Supply Service

Fsuppl., Federal Supplement

FTC, Federal Trade Commission

FWS, Fish and Wildlife Service

GAO, General Accounting Office

GAR, Grand Army of the Republic

GARIOA, Government and Relief in Occupied Areas

GATT, General Agreement on Tariffs and Trade

GAW, guaranteed annual wage

GCA, ground-control approach

GCD or **gcd,** greatest common divisor

GCI, ground control intercept

GCT, Greenwich Civil Time

GI, gastrointestinal, general issue, Government issue

GMAT, Greenwich Mean Astronomical Time

GM & S, general, medical, and surgical

GMT, Greenwich Mean Time

GNMA, Government National Mortgage Association (Ginnie Mae)

GNP, gross national product

GPO, Government Printing Office

gr. Wt., gross weight

GS, Geological Survey

GSA, General Services Administration

GTS, gas turbine ship

HC, House of Commons

hcf, highest common factor

H Con. Res. (with number), House concurrent resolution

H Doc. (with number), House document

HE, high explosive

HHFA, Housing and Home Finance Agency

HHS, or **DHHS,** Department of Health and Human Services

HJ Res (with number), House joint resolution

HL, House of Lords

Hosp. Steward, hospital steward

How., Howard (U.S. Supreme Court Reports)

HR or **H.R.** (with numbers), House bill

H Rept. (with number), House report

H Res. (with number), House resolution

HUD, Department of Housing and Urban Development

IADB, Inter-American Defense Board

IAEA, International Atomic Energy Agency

ICBM, intercontinental ballistic missile

ICC, Interstate Commerce Commission, Indian Claims Commission

id, inside diameter

IDA, International Development Association

IF, infield, intermediate frequency

IFC, International Finance Corporation

IFF, Identification, Friend or Foe

ILO, International Labor Organization

IMCO, Intergovernmental Maritime Consultative Organization
IMF, International Monetary Fund
INS, Immigration and Naturalization Service
Insp. Gen., Inspector General
Interpol, International Criminal Police Organization
IOU, I owe you
IQ, intelligence quotient
IRAC, Interdepartment Radio Advisory Committee
IRBM, intermediate range ballistic missile
IRE, Institute of Radio Engineers
IRO, International Refugee Organization
IRS, International Revenue Service
ITO, International Trade Organization
ITU, International Telecommunication Union, International Typographical Union
JAG, Judge Advocate General
jato or **JATO,** jet-assisted takeoff
JD. *jurum doctor*, doctor of laws
JOBS, Job Opportunities in the Business Sector
Judge Adv. Gen., Judge Advocate General
KCB, Knight Commander of the Bath
LAFTA, Latin American Free Trade Association
lat. or **lat,** latitude
LC, Library of Congress
lc, lowercase
lcl, less-than-carload lot
lcm, least common multiple
LEd., Lawyer's edition (U.S. Supreme Court Reports)

LitD or **Lit.D,** Doctor of Literature
LLB or **LL.B.,** Bachelor of Laws
LLD or **LL.D.,** Doctor of Laws
log, logarithm
long or **long.,** longitude
loran, long-range navigation
lox or **LOX,** liquid oxygen
LPG, liquefied petroleum gas
LST, Local Standard Time
LT, Local Time
LTL, less than truckload
lwl, load waterline
lwm, low watermark
MA or **M.A.,** Master of Arts, Maritime Administration, Manpower Administration
MAC, Military Airlift Command (formerly MATS)
maf, moisture and ash free (coal)
MAG, Military Advisory Group
MB, Manitoba, megabyte
MC or **M.C.,** Member of Congress, emcee (master of ceremonies)
MCA, Model Cities Administration
MD or **M.D.,** Doctor of Medicine, Medical Department
MDAP, Mutual Defense Assistance Program
mf, machine finish, medium frequency
Misc. Doc. (with number), miscellaneous document
mmf, magnetomotive force
mol wt, molecular weight
MOS, military occupational specialty

MP or **M.P.,** Member of Parliament, Military Police, Mounted Police

mp, melting point

MS, or **M.S.,** or **MSc,** or **M.Sc.,** Master of Science

MSC, Military Sealift Command

msl, mean sea level

MST, Mountain Standard Time

MT, Mountain Time

N, normal

NA, not available

NAC, national agency check

NAS, National Academy of Science

NASA, National Aeronautics and Space Administration

NATO, North Atlantic Treaty Organization

NB, New Brunswick

NBS, National Bureau of Standards

NCUA, National Credit Union Administration

nec, not elsewhere classified

nes, not elsewhere specified

net wt., net weight

NF, Newfoundland, National Formulary

NFAH, National Foundation on the Arts and the Humanities

n-fe, nitrogen-free extract

NFSN, French-Speaking Nations of NATO

NIH, National Institutes of Health

nl, natural log or logarithm

NLRB, National Labor Relations Board

NOAA, National Oceanic and Atmospheric Administration

noibn, not otherwise indexed by name

nop, not otherwise provided (for)

nos, not otherwise specified

NOS, National Ocean Survey (formerly Coast and Geodetic Survey)

NOVS, National Office of Vital Statistic

NPS, National Park Service

NS, naval station, new series, New Style, Nova Scotia, nuclear ship

NSA, National Shipping Authority

NSC, National Security Council

NSF, National Science Foundation

nsk, not specified by kind

nspf, not specifically provided for

NT or **N.T.,** New Testament, Northern Territory, Northwest Territories

OASDHI, Old-Age, Survivors, Disability, and Health Insurance Program

OASI, Old-Age and Survivors Insurance

OCD, Office of Civil Defense

OD or **O.D.,** Doctor Optometry, Officer of the Day

od, olive drab, outside diameter

OE, Office of Education

OEO, Office of Economic Opportunity

OEP, Office of Emergency Preparedness, Office of Emergency Planning

OIT, Office of International Trade

OK, OK'd, OK'ing, OK's

OMB, Office of Management and Budget (formerly **BOB,** Bureau of the Budget)

ON, Old Norse, Ontario

OSD, Office of the Secretary of Defense

OTC, Organization for Trade Cooperation

PA, physician assistant, Post Adjutant, power of attorney, public-address system

Passed Asst. Surg., Passed Assistant Surgeon

PBS, Public Broadcasting Service

PE, physical education, Prince Edward Island

Pet, Peters (US Supreme Court Reports)

Ph, phenyl

ph, phase

PHA, Public Housing Administration

Phar D, Doctor of Pharmacy

PhB or **BPh,** Bachelor of Philosophy

PhD or **Ph.D.,** Doctor of Philosophy

PhG, Graduate in Pharmacy

PHS, Public Health Service

pl or **pl.,** plate, plural

PO Box (with number), *but* post office box (in general sense)

pod, pay on delivery

por, pay on return

POW, prisoner of war

PP, parcel post, postpaid, prepaid

PPI, plan position indicator

ppi, policy proof of interest

pq, previous question
PQ, Province of Quebec
Private Res. (with number), private resolution
PST, Pacific Standard Time
PT, Pacific Time
PTA, Parent-Teacher Association
pto, please turn over
Public Res. (with number), public resolution
PX, Post Exchange
QT, on the quiet
racon, radar beacon
radar, radio detection and ranging
R & D, research and development
rato, rocket-assisted takeoff
RB, Renegotiation Board
RDB, Research and Development Board
REA, Rural Electrification Administration
Rev., Revelation, Reverend
Rev. Stat., Revised Statutes
rf, radio frequency
RFD or **R.F.D.,** Rural Free Delivery
Rh, Rhesus (blood factor)
RN or **R.N.,** Registered Nurse, Royal Navy
ROP, run of paper
ROTC, Reserve Officer's Training Corps
RR or **R.R.,** railroad, Right Reverend, Rural Route
RRB, Railroad Retirement Board
Rwy or **Rwy.,** Railway
SAC, Strategic Air Command

SACEUR, Supreme Allied Commander Europe
SAE, Society of Automotive Engineers
SAGE, semiautomatic ground environment
s and sc, sized and supercalendered
SAR, Sons of the American Revolution
SBA, Small Business Administration
SCAP, Supreme Commander of the Allied Powers (Japan)
S Con. Res. (with number), Senate Concurrent Resolution
S Doc. (with number), Senate document
SEATO, Southeast Asia Treaty Organization
SEC, Securities and Exchange Commission
sec or **sec.,** secant, seconds, secondary, secretary, section
sech, hyperbolic secant
2d, 3d, second, third
ser., series, sermon
Sf, Svedberg floatation
SHAPE, Supreme Headquarters Allied Powers (Europe)
SHF, superhigh frequency
shoran, short range (radio)
SI, Systeme International d' Unites
sin, sine
sinh, hyperbolic sine
SJ Res (with number), Senate Joint Resolution
SK, Saskatchewan
so, seller's option

sofar, sound fixing and ranging
sonar, sound, navigation, and ranging
SOP or **S.O.P.,** standard operating procedure
SOS, wireless distress signal
SP, Shore Patrol, Submarine Patrol
SPAR, Coast Guard Women's Reserve (*Semper Paratus—Always Ready*)
sp gr or **sp. gr.,** specific gravity
S Rept. (with number), Senate Report
S Res. (with number), Senate Resolution
SRS, Social and Rehabilitation Service
SS or **S.S.,** Social Security, steamship
SSA, Social Security Administration
SSS, Selective Service System
St., Saint, Strait, Street
Ste., SS., Sainte, Saints
Stat., Statutes at Large
STP, standard temperature and pressure
SUNFED, Special United Nations Fund for Economic Development
Sup. Ct., Supreme Court Reporter
Supp. Rev. Stat., Supplement to the Revised Statutes
Surg. Gen., Surgeon General
tan, tangent
tanh, hyperbolic tangent
TB, tuberculosis
TD, touchdown, Treasury Department, Treasury Decisions
TDN, total digestible nutrients

ter., terrace, territory
tlo, total loss only
tm, true mean
TNT, trinitrotoluene
TOFC, trailer-on-flatcar
Tp., township
TV, television
TVA, Tennessee Valley Authority
2,4-D, insecticide
uc., upper case
UHF or **uhf,** ultrahigh frequency
UMTS, Universal Military Training Service (or System)
UN, United Nations
UNESCO, United Nations Educational, Scientific, and Cultural Organization
UNICEF, United Nations Children's Fund
URA, Urban Renewal Administration
USA or **U.S.A.,** United States of America, US Army
USAF, US Air Force
USAREUR, US Army, Europe
USC, United States Code
USCA, United States Code Annotated
USC Suppl, United States Code Supplement
USCG, US Coast Guard
USDA, United States Department of Agriculture
USES, US Employment Service
USIA, US Information Agency
USMC, US Marine Corps

USN, US Navy

USNR, US Naval Reserve

USP or **U.S.P.,** United States Pharmacopoeia

USS, US Senate, US ship

USSR or **U.S.S.R.,** Union of Soviet Socialist Republics

ut, universal time

VA, Veterans' Administration

VAR, visual-aural range

VCR, video cassette recorder

VHF, very high frequency

VIP, very important person (see also **DV**)

VLF or **vlf,** very low frequency

WAC, Women's Army Corps

wae, when actually employed

WAF, Women in the Air Force

Wall, Wallace (US Supreme Court Reports)

WAVES, Women Accepted for Volunteer Emergency Service

wf, wrong font

Wheat., Wheaton (US Supreme Court Reports)

WHO, World Health Organization

wi, when issued

WMAL, WRC, etc., radio stations

woc, without compensation

YT, Yukon Territory

ZIP Code, zone improvement plan code (Postal Service)

METRIC ABBREVIATIONS

Metric abbreviations are typed in lowercase, the same form being used for both singular and plural. The preferred abbreviation for *cubic centimeter* is cm^3, rather than *cc*.

Prefixes for Multiples and Submultiples			
T	tera (10^{12})	c	centi (10^{-2})
G	giga (10^9)	m	milli (10^{-3})
M	mega (10^6)	µ	micro (10^{-6})
k	kilo (10^3)	n	nano (10^{-9})
h	hecto(10^2)	p	pico (10^{-12})
da	deka (10)	f	femto (10^{-15})
d	deci (10^{-1})	a	atto (10^{-18})

Length		Area	
m	meter	m^2	square meter
mym	myriameter	mya	myriare
km	kilometer	km^2	square kilometer
hm	hectometer	hm^2	square hectometer
dam	dekameter	dam^2	square dekameter

Length		Area	
dm	decimeter	dm^2	square decimeter
cm	centimeter	cm^2	square centimeter
mm	millimeter	mm^2	square millimeter

Volume		Weight	
m3	cubic meter	g	gram
km3	cubic kilometer	myg	myriagram
hm3	cubic hectometer	kg	kilogram
dam3	cubic dekameter	hg	hectogram
dm3	cubic decimeter	dag	dekagram
cm3	cubic centimeter	dg	decigram
mm3	cubic millimeter	cg	centigram
		mg	milligram
		μg	microgram

Land Area		Capacity of Containers	
a	are	l	liter
ha	hectare	myl	myrialiter
ca	centiare	kl	kiloliter

Land Area	Capacity of Containers	
	hl	hectoliter
	dal	dekaliter
	dl	deciliter
	cl	centiliter
	ml	milliliter

A similar plan of abbreviation applies to any unit based on the metric system:

A	ampere	V	volt
Å	angstrom	W	Watt
c	cycle (radio)	kc	kilocycle
dyn	dyne	kV	kilovolt
erg	erg	kVA	kilovolt-ampere
F	farad	kW	kilowatt
H	henry	mF	millifarad
J	joule	mH	millihenry
mho	(not abbreviated)	μF	microfarad (one mil-lionth of a farad)
ohm	(not abbreviated)		

STANDARD ABBREVIATIONS FOR OTHER UNITS OF MEASURE

a, are (unit of area), atto (prefix, one-quintillionth)
aA, attoampere
abs, absolute (temperature and gravity)
AF or **af,** audio-frequency
AM, amplitude modulation
asb, apostilb
at, atmosphere, technical
atm, atmosphere (infrequently, A_s)
at wt, atomic weight
avdp., avoirdupois
b, barn, bit
B, bel
bbl, barrel
bbl/d, barrel per day
Bd, baud
bd ft, board foot
Bhn, Brinell hardness number
bhp, brake horsepower
bm, board measure
bp, boiling point
Btu's or **BTU'S,** British thermal units
bu, bushel
C, coulomb, Celsius (preferred), also Centigrade
C or **C.** or **c** or **¢** or **ct,** cent
°C, degree Celsius
cal, calorie

cal., caliber
cd, candela
cd-ft, cord-foot
cd/in^2, candela per square inch
cd/m^2, candela per square meter
cfm, cubic feet per minute
cfs, cubic feet per second
c-h, candle-hour
Ci, curie
cp, candle power
cP, centipoise
cSt, centistokes
cu ft (obsolete), see **ft3**
cu in (obsolete), see **in3**
cu yd (obsolete), see **yd3**
cwt, hundredweight
D, darcy
d, day, degree, diameter, penny, pence, deci (prefix, one-tenth)
db or **dB,** decibel
dbu, decibel unit
dol, dollar
doz or **doz.,** dozen(s)
dr, dram
dwt, deadweight tons
EHF or **ehf,** extremely high frequency
EMF or **emf,** electromotive force
esu, electrostatic unit
°F, degree Fahrenheit

F, Fahrenheit; femi
fbm, feet board measure
fc, foot-candle
fL, footlambert
FM, frequency modulation
ft or **ft.,** foot, feet
ft^2, square foot
ft^3, cubic foot
ftH$_2$0, conventional foot of water
ft-lb, foot-pound
ft-lbf, foot pound-force
ft/min, foot per minute
ft^2/min, square foot per minute
ft^3/min, cubic foot per minute
ft-pdl, foot poundal
ft/s, foot per second
ft^2/s, square foot per second
ft^3/s, cubic foot per second
ft/s^2, foot per second squared
ft/s^3, foot per second cubed
G, gauss, giga (prefix, 1 billion), gravity
Gal, gal (acceleration)
gal or **gal.,** gallon
gal/min, gallons per minute
gal/s, gallons per second
Gb, gilbert
g/cm^3, gram per cubic centimeter
GeV, giga-electron-volt
GHz, gigahertz, gigacycle per second

gr, grain, gram, gross
h, hour, hecto (prefix, 100)
ha, hectare
hf, half, high frequency
HP or **hp,** horsepower
hph, horsepowerhour
Hz, hertz (cycles per second)
ihp, indicated horsepower
in, inch
in^2, square inch
in^3, cubic inch
in/h, inch per hour
inH2O, conventional inch of water
inHg, conventional inch of mercury
in-lb, inch-pound
in/s, inch per second
K, karat, kayser, kilobyte, Kelvin (no degree symbol °)
k, karat, kilo (prefix, 1,000)
kHz or **khz,** kilohertz (kilocycles per second)
klbf, kilopound-force
kt, karat, kiloton, knot
L, lambert
lb or **lb.,** pound(s)
lb ap, apothecary, pound
lb, avdp, avoirdupois, pound
lbf, pound-force
lbf/ft, pound-force foot
lbf/ft^2, pound-force per square foot
lfg/ft^3, pound-force per cubic foot

lbf/in^2, pound-force per square inch
lb/ft, pound per foot
lb/ft^2, pound per square foot
lb/ft^3, pound per cubic foot
lb/in^{2}a, pounds per square inch absolute
lb/in^{2}g, pounds per square inch gage
lct, long calcined ton
ldt, long dry ton
LF or **lf,** low frequency
lin ft, linear foot
l/m, lines per minute
lm, lumen
lm/ft^2, lumen per square foot
lm/m^2, lumen per square meter
lm-s, lumen second
lm/W, lumen per watt
l/s, lines per second
l/s, liter per second
lx, lux
M, Roman numeral for 1,000
M#bm, thousand (feet) board measure
mD, millidarcy
meq, milliequivalent
M#ft^3, thousand cubic feet
Mgal/d, million gallons per day
MHz or **Mhz,** megahertz
mHz, millihertz
mi or **mi.,** mile
mi^2, square mile

mi/h, mile per hour
min., minute (time)
mol, mole (unit of substance)
ms, millisecond
MT, megaton
Mx, maxwell
N, newton
N•m, newton meter
N/m^2, newton per square meter
nmi, nautical mile
Np, neper
ns, nanosecond
N•s/m^2, newton second per square meter
nt, nit
Oe, oersted (use of **A/m,** amperes permeter, preferred)
oz or **oz.,** ounce(s)
P, poise
Pa, pascal
pct, percent
pdl, poundal
pF, water-holding energy
pH, hydrogen-ion concentration
ph, phot
pk, peck
p/m, parts per million
ps, picosecond
pt or **pt.,** pint(s)
pwt, pennyweight

ql, quintal
qt or **qt.,** quart(s)
R, rankine; roentgen
°R, degree rankine; degree reaumur
rad, radian
rd, rad
rem, rem
rms, root mean square
rpm, revolutions per minute
rps, revolutions per second
s or **s.,** second(s) (time)
S, siemens
sb, stilb
scp, spherical candlepower
s-ft, second-foot
shp, shaft horsepower
slug, slug
sr, steradian
sSf, standard saybolt fural
sSu, standard saybolt universal
stdft^3, standard cubic foot (feet)
Sus, saybolt universal second
t or **t.,** ton
tbs or **tbs.** or **tbsp** or **tbsp.,** tablespoon
thm, therm
Twad, twaddell
u (unified), atomic mass unit
var, var
VHF or **vhf,** very high frequency

Wb, weber
W/sr, watt per steradian
W/(sr•m^2), watt per steradian square meter
yd or **yd.,** yard(s)
yd^2, square yard
yd^3, cubic yard
yr or **yr.,** year(s)

LATIN ABBREVIATIONS

a., *annus,* year; *ante,* before
A.A.C., *anno ante Christum,* in the year before Christ
A.A.S., *Academiae Americanae Socius,* Fellow of the American Academy [Academy of Arts and Sciences]
AB or **A.B.,** *artium baccalaureus,* bachelor of arts
ab init., *ab initio,* from the beginning
abs. re., *absente reo,* the defendant being absent
AC or **A.C.,** *ante Christum,* before Christ
AD or **A.D.,** *anno Domini,* in the year of our Lord
a.d., *ante diem,* before the day
ad fin., *ad finem,* at the end, to one end
ad h.l., *ad hunc locum,* to this place, on this passage
ad inf., *ad infinitum,* to infinity
ad init., *ad initium,* at the beginning
ad int., *ad interim,* in the meantime
ad lib., *ad libitum,* at pleasure
ad loc., *ad locum,* at the place
ad val., *ad valorem,* according to value

A.I., *anno inventionis,* in the year of the discovery

al., *alia, alii,* other things, other persons

AM or **A.M.,** *anno mundi,* in the year of the world; *Annus mirabilis,* the wonderful year [1666]; a.m., *ante meridiem,* before noon

an., *anno,* in the year; *ante,* before

ann., *annales,* annals; *anni,* years

A.R.S.S., *Antiquariorum Regiae Societatis Socius,* Fellow of the Royal Society of Antiquaries

A.U.C., *anno urbis conditae, ab urbe condita,* in [the year from] the building of the City [Rome], 753 B.C.

BA or **B.A.,** *baccalaureus artium,* bachelor of arts

BS or **B. Sc.,** *baccalaureus scientiae,* bachelor of science

C., *centum,* a hundred; *condemno,* I condemn, find guilty

c., *circa,* about

cent., *centum,* a hundred

cf., *confer,* compare

CM or **C.M.,** *chirurgiae magister,* master of surgery

coch., *cochlear,* a spoon, spoonful

coch. amp., *cochlear amplum,* a tablespoonful

coch. mag., *cochlear magnum,* a large spoonful

coch. med., *cochlear medium,* a dessert spoonful

coch. parv., *cochlear parvum,* a teaspoonful

con., *contra,* against; *conjunx,* wife

C.P.S., *custos privati sigilli,* keeper of the privy seal

C.S., *custos sigilli,* keeper of the seal

D., *Deus,* God; *Dominus,* Lord; d., *decretum,* a decree; *denarius,* a penny; *da,* give

DD or **D.D.,** *divinitatis doctor,* doctor of divinity

D.G., *Dei gratia,* by the grace of God; *Deo gratias,* thanks to God

D.N., *Dominus noster,* our Lord

DSc or **D.Sc.,** *doctor scientiae,* doctor of science

d.s.p., *decessit sine prole,* died without issue

D.V., *Deo volente,* God willing

e.g., *exempli gratia,* for example

et al., *et alibi,* and elsewhere; *et alii,* or *aliae,* and others

etc., *et cetera,* and others, and so forth

et seq., *et sequentes,* and those that follow

et ux., *et uxor,* and wife

F., *filius,* son

f., *fiat,* let it be made; *forte,* strong

fac., *factum similis,* facsimile, an exact copy

fasc., *fasciculus,* a bundle

fl., *flores,* flowers; *floruit,* flourished; *fluidus,* fluid

f.r., *folio recto,* right-hand page

F.R.S., *Franternitatis Regiae Socius,* Fellow of the Royal Society

f.v., *folio verso,* on the back of the leaf

guttat., *guttatim,* by drops

H., *hora,* hour

h.a., *hoc anno,* in this year; *hujus anni,* this year's

hab. corp., *habeas corpus,* have the body—a writ

h.e., *hic est,* this is; *hoc est,* that is

h.m., *hoc mense,* in the month; *huius mensis,* this month's

h.q., *hoc quaere,* look for this

H.R.I.P., *hic requiescat in pace,* here rests in peace

H.S., *hic sepultus,* here is buried; *hic situs,* here lies; h.s., *hoc sensu,* in this sense

H.S.S., *Historiae Societatis Socius,* Fellow of the Historical Soecity

h.t., *hoc tempore,* at this time; *hoc titulo,* in or under this title

I., *Idus,* the Ides; i., *id,* that; *immortalis,* immortal

ib. or **ibid.,** *ibidem,* in the same place

id., *idem,* the same

i.e., *id est,* that is

imp., *imprimatur, sanction,* let it be printed

I.N.D., *in nomine Dei,* in the name of God

in f., *in fine,* at the end

inf., *infra,* below

init., *initio,* in the beginning

in lim., *in limine,* on the threshold, at the outset

in loc., *in loco,* in its place

in loc. cit., *in loco citato,* in the place cited

in pr., *in principio,* in the beginning

in trans., *in transitu,* on the way

i.q., *idem quod,* the same as

i.q.e.d., *id quod erat demonstrandum,* what was to be proved

J., *judex,* judge

JCD or **J.C.D.,** *juris civilis doctor,* doctor of civil law

JD or **J.D.,** *jurum doctor,* doctor of laws

JUD or **J.U.D.,** *juris utriusque doctor,* doctor of both civil and canon law

L., *liber,* a book; *locus,* a place

L, *libra,* pound; placed before figures, thus L10; if l., to be placed after, as 40l.

LAM or **L.A.M.,** *liberalium artium magister,* master of the liberal arts

LB or **L.B.,** *baccalaureus literarum,* bachelor of letters

lb., *libra,* pound (singular and plural)

LHD or **L.H.D.,** *literarum humaniorum doctor,* doctor of the more humane letters

LittD or **Litt. D.** or **Dlit(t),** *literarum doctor,* doctor of letters

LLB or **LL.B.,** *legum baccalaureus,* bachelor of laws

LLD or **LL.D.,** *legum doctor,* doctor of laws

LLM or **LL.M.,** *legum magister,* master of laws

loc. cit., *loco citato,* in the place cited

loq., *loquitur,* he, or she, speaks

L.S., *locus sigilli,* the place of the seal

l.s.c., *loco supra citato,* in the place above cited

L s.d., *librae, solidi, denarii,* pounds, shillings, pence

M., *magister,* master; *manipulus,* handful; *medicinae,* of medicine

m., *meridies,* noon

MA or **M.A.,** *magister artium,* master of arts

MB or **M.B.,** *medicinae baccalaureus,* bachelor of medicine

MCh or **M.Ch.,** *magister chirurgiae,* master of surgery

MD or **M.D.,** *medicinae doctor,* doctor of medicine

m.m., *mutatis mutandis,* with the necessary changes

m.n., *mutato nomine,* the name being changed

MS., *manuscriptum,* manuscript; MSS., *manuscripta,* manuscripts

MusB or **Mus. B.,** *musicae baccalaureus,* bachelor of music

MusD or **Mus. D.,** *musicae doctor,* doctor of music

MusM or **Mus. M.,** *musicae magister,* master of music

N., *Nepos,* grandson; *nomen,* name; *nomina,* names; *noster,* our; n., *natus,* born; *nocte,* at night

N.B., *nota bene,* mark well

ni. pri., *nisi prius,* unless before

nob., *nobis,* for (or on) our part

nol. pros., *nolle prosequi,* will not prosecute

non cul., *non culpabilis,* not guilty

n.l., *non licet,* it is not permitted; *non liquet,* it is not clear; *non longe,* not far

non obs., *non obstante,* notwithstanding

non pros., *non prosequitur,* he does not prosecute

non seq., *non sequitur,* it does not follow logically

O., *octarius,* a pint

ob., *obiit,* he, or she, died; *obiter,* incidentally

ob. s.p., *obiit sine prole,* died without issue

o.c., *opere citato,* in the work cited

op., *opus,* work; *opera,* works

op. cit., *opere citato,* in the work cited

P., *papa,* pope; *pater,* father; *pontifex,* bishop; *populus,* people; p., *partim,* in part; *per,* by, for; *pius,* holy; *pondere,* by weight; *post,* after; *primus,* first; *pro,* for

p.a. or **per ann.,** *per annum,* yearly; *pro anno,* for the year

p. ae., *partes aequales,* equal parts

pass., *passim,* everywhere

percent., *per centum,* by the hundred

pil., *pilula,* pill

PhB or **Ph.B.,** *philosophiae baccalaureus,* bachelor of philosophy

pm or **p.m.,** *post mortem,* after death

PM or **P.M.,** *post meridem,* afternoon

pro tem., *pro tempore,* for the time being

prox., *proximo,* in or of the next [month]

P.S., *postscriptum,* postscript; P.SS., *post scripta,* postscripts

q.d., *quasi dicat,* as if one should say; *quais dictum,* as if said; *quasi dixisset,* as if he had said

q.e., *quod est,* which is

Q.E.D., *quod erat demonstrandum,* which was to be demonstrated

Q.E.F., *quod erat faciendum,* which was to be done

Q.E.I., *quod erat inveniendum,* which was to be found out

q.l., *quantum libet,* as much as you please

q. pl., *quantum placet,* as much as seems good

q.s., *quantum sufficit,* sufficient quantity

q.v., *quantum vis,* as much as you will; *quem, quam, quod vide,* which see; qq. v., *quos, quas,* or *quae vide,* which see (plural)

R., *regina,* queen; *recto,* right-hand page; *respublica,* commonwealth

R, *recipe,* take

R.I.P., *requiescat,* or *requiescant, in pace,* may he, she, or they, rest in peace

R.P.D., *rerum politicarum doctor,* doctor of political science

t. or **temp.,** *tempore,* in the time of

tal. qual., *talis qualis,* just as they come, average quality

R.S.S., *Ragiae Societatis Sodalis,* Fellow of the Royal Society

S., *sepultus,* buried; *situs,* lies; *societas,* society; *socius* or *sodalis,* fellow; s., *semi,* half; *solidus,* shilling

s.a., *sine anno,* without date; *secundum artem,* according to art

S.A.S., *Societatis Antiquariorum Socius,* Fellow of the Society of Antiquaries

sc., *scilicet,* namely; *sculpsit,* he, or she, carved or engraved it

ScB or **Sc.B.,** *scientiae baccalaureus,* bachelor of science

ScD or **Sc.D.,** *scientiae doctor,* doctor of science

S.D., *salutem dicit,* sends greetings

s.d., *sine die,* indefinitely

sec., *secundum,* according to

sec. leg., *secundum legem,* according to law

sec. nat., *secundum naturam,* according to nature, or naturally

sec. reg., *secundum regulam,* according to rule

seq., *sequens, sequentes, sequentia,* the following

S.H.S., *Societatis Historiae Socius,* Fellow of the Historical Society

s.h.v., *sub hac voce* or *sub hoc verbo,* under this word

s.l.a.n., *sine loco, anno, vel nomine,* without place, date or name

s.l.p., *sine legitima prole,* without lawful issue

s.m.p., *sine mascula prole,* without male issue

s.n., *sine nomine,* without name

s.p., *sine prole,* without issue

S.P.A.S., *Societatis Philosophiae Americanae Socius,* Fellow of the American Philosophical Society

s.p.s., *sine prole superstite,* without surviving issue

S.R.S., *Societatis Regiae Socius or Sodalis,* Fellow of the Royal Society

ss., *scilicet,* namely (in law)

S.S.C., *Societas Sanctae Crucis,* Society of the Holy Cross

stat., *statim,* immediately

STB or **S.T.B.,** *sacrae theologiae baccalaureus,* bachelor of sacred theology

STD or **S.T.D.,** *sacrae theologiae doctor,* doctor of sacred theology

STP or **S.T.P.,** *sacrae theologiae professor,* professor of sacred theology

sub., *subaudi,* understand, supply

sup., *supra,* above

both civil and canon law

ult., *ultimo,* last month (may be abbreviated in writing but should be spelled out in printing)

ung., *unguentum,* ointment

u.s., *ubi supra,* in the place above mentioned

ut dict., *ut dictum,* as directed

ut sup., *ut supra,* as above

ux., *uxor,* wife

v. or **vs.,** *versus,* against; *vide,* see; *voce,* voice, word

v.—a., *vixit—annos,* lived [so many] years

verb. sap., *verbum [satis] sapienti,* a word to the wise suffices

v.g., *verbi gratia,* for example

viz., *videlicet,* namely

v.s., *vide supra,* see above

FORMS OF ADDRESS

The following are conventional forms of address in general use. They may be varied where appropriate. Use them as guides for other addresses.

All presidential and federal and state elective officials are addressed as *Honorable*. A person once entitled to *Governor, Judge, General, Honorable* or a similar distinctive title may retain the title for his or her lifetime.

When a woman occupies the position, substitute *Ms.* for *Mr.* However, before such formal titles as *President, Vice President, Chairman, Secretary, Ambassador,* or *Minister,* use *Madam* or *Mme.* If in doubt err on the side of formality and use *Mme.* Use the title *Senator* for a female member of the Senate and *Ms.* for a female member of the House of Representatives, Senator-elect, or Representative-elect.

In most States, the lower branch of the legislature is the House of Representatives. In some States, such as California, New York, New Jersey, Nevada, and Wisconsin, the lower house is known as the Assembly. In others, such as Maryland, Virginia, and West

Virginia, it is known as the House of Delegates. Nebraska has a one-house legislature. Its members are classed as Senators.

Academic or professional titles replace *Mr.* or *Ms.* Don't use two titles with the same meaning with one name: write *Dr. Paula White* or *Paula White, MD,* not *Dr. Paula White, MD* or *Ms. Paula White, MD.* Spell out all titles in an address except *Dr., Mr., Mrs.,* and *Ms.* Use *Ms.* for women generally, unless the woman addressed has expressed a preference for *Miss* or *Mrs.*

The term *pastor* applies to a minister who leads a congregation. It is appropriately used in conversation or direct address, but not in formal, written address.

Addressee	Address on Letter and Envelope	Salutation and Complimentary Close
The President	The President The White House Washington, DC 20500	Dear Mr./Mme. President: Respectfully,
Spouse of the President	Mr./Mrs. (full name) The White House Washington, DC 20500	Dear Mr./Mrs. (surname): Sincerely,
Assistant to the President	Honorable (full name) Assistant to the President The White House Washington, DC 20500	Dear Mr./Ms. (surname): Sincerely,

Addressee	Address on Letter and Envelope	Salutation and Complimentary Close
The Vice-President	The Vice-President United States Senate Washington, DC 20510	Dear Mr./Mme. Vice-President Sincerely,
The Chief Justice	The Chief Justice of the United States The Supreme Court of the United States Washington, DC 20543	Dear Mr./Mme. Chief Justice: or Dear Chief Justice (surname): Sincerely,
Associate Justice	Mr./Mme. Justice (surname) The Supreme Court of the United States Washington, DC 20543	Dear Mr./Mme. Justice or Dear Justice (surname): Sincerely,

United States Senator	Honorable (full name) United States Senate Washington, DC 20510 *or* Honorable (full name) United States Senator (local address) 00000	Dear Senator (surname): Sincerely,
United States Representative	Honorable (full name) House of Representatives Washington, DC 20515 *or* Honorable (full name) Member, United States House of Representatives (local address) 00000	Dear Mr./Ms. (surname): Sincerely,

307

Addressee	Address on Letter and Envelope	Salutation and Complimentary Close
Committee Chairman	Honorable (full name) Chairman, Committee on (name) United States Senate Washington, DC 20510 *or* Honorable (full name) Chairman, Committee on (name) House of Representatives Washington, DC 20515	Dear Mr./Mme. Chairman: Sincerely,

Subcommittee Chairman	Honorable (full name)	Dear Senator
	Chairman, Subcommittee on (name)	(surname):
	(name of parent Committee)	Sincerely,
	United States Senate	
	Washington, DC 20510	
	or	
	Honorable (full name)	Dear Mr./Mme.
	Chairman, Subcommittee on (name)	(surname):
	House of Representatives	Sincerely,
	Washington, DC 20515	

309

Addressee	Address on Letter and Envelope	Salutation and Complimentary Close
Speaker of the House of Representatives	Honorable (full name) Speaker of the House of Representatives Washington, DC 20515	Dear Mr./Ms. Speaker: Sincerely,
Cabinet Members	Honorable (full name) Secretary of (name of Department) Washington, DC 00000 *or* Honorable (full name) Postmaster General Washington, DC 20260	Dear Mr./Mme. Secretary: Sincerely, Dear Mr./Ms. Postmaster General: Sincerely,

	or	
	Honorable (full name) Attorney General Washington, DC 20530	Dear Mr./Ms. Attorney General: Sincerely,
Deputy Secretaries, Assistants, or Under Secretaries	Honorable (full name) Deputy Secretary of (name of department) Washington, DC 00000	Dear Mr./Mme. (surname): Sincerely,
	or	
	Honorable (full name) Assistant Secretary of (name of Department) Washington, DC 00000	

311

312

Addressee	Address on Letter and Envelope	Salutation and Complimentary Close
	or	
	Honorable (full name) Under Secretary of (name of Department) Washington, DC 00000	
Head of Independent Offices and Agencies	Honorable (full name) Comptroller General of the United States General Accounting Office Washington, DC 20548	Dear Mr./Ms. (surname): Sincerely,

	or	
	Honorable (full name) Chairman, (name of Commission) Washington, DC 00000	Dear Mr./Mme. Chairman: Sincerely,
	or	
	Honorable (full name) Director, Bureau of the Budget Washington, DC 20503	Dear Mr./Ms. (surname): Sincerely,
Librarian of Congress	Honorable (full name) Librarian of Congress Library of Congress Washington, DC 20540	Dear Mr./Ms. (surname): Sincerely,

Addressee	Address on Letter and Envelope	Salutation and Complimentary Close
Public Printer	Honorable (full name) Public Printer US Government Printing Office Washington, DC 20401	Dear Mr./Ms. (surname): Sincerely,
American Ambassador	Honorable (full name) American Ambassador (City), (Country)	Sir/Madam: (formal) Dear Mr./Mme. Ambassador: (informal) Very truly yours, (formal) Sincerely, (informal)

American Consul General or American Consul	(Full name) American Consul General (or American Consul) (City), (Country)	Dear Mr./Ms. (surname): Sincerely,
Foreign Ambassador in the United States	His Excellency (full name) Ambassador of (Country) (local address) 0000	Excellency (formal) Dear Mr./Mme. Ambassador: (informal) Very truly yours, (formal) Sincerely, (informal)

Addressee	Address on Letter and Envelope	Salutation and Complimentary Close
United States Representative to the United Nations or Organization of American States	Honorable (full name) United States Representative to the United Nations (or Organization of American States) (local address) 00000	Sir/Madame: (formal) Dear Mr./Mme. Ambassador: (informal) Very truly yours, (formal) Sincerely, (informal)
Governor of State	Honorable (full name) Governor of (name of State) (City), (State) 00000	Dear Governor (surname): Sincerely,

Lieutenant Governor	Honorable (full name) Lieutenant Governor of (name of State) (City), (State) 00000	Dear Mr./Ms. (surname): Sincerely,
State Senator	Honorable (full name) (name of State) Senate (City), (State) 00000	Dear Mr./Ms. (surname): Sincerely,
State Representative, Assemblyman, or Delegate	Honorable (full name) (name of State) House of Representatives (or Assembly or House of Delegates) (City), (State) 00000	Dear Mr./Ms. (surname): Sincerely,

Addressee	Address on Letter and Envelope	Salutation and Complimentary Close
Mayor	Honorable (full name) Mayor of (name of City) (City), (State) 00000	Dear Mayor (surname): Sincerely,
President of a Board of Commissioners	Honorable (full name) President, Board of Commissioners of (name of City) (City), (State) 00000	Dear Mr./Ms. (surname): Sincerely,
Protestant Clergy Episcopalian	The Most Reverend Archbishop of (Canterbury or York) (local address) 00000	Most Reverend Sir: (full name) (formal) Dear Archbishop (surname): (informal) Sincerely,

Episcopalian	The Right Reverend Bishop of (Church) (local address) 00000	Right Reverend Sir: (full name) (formal) Dear Bishop (surname): (informal) Sincerely,
Lutheran ⎤ Methodist ⎦	The Reverend (full name) Bishop of (name) (local address) 00000	Reverend Sir/Madam: (formal) Dear Bishop (surname): (informal) Sincerely,

Addressee	Address on Letter and Envelope	Salutation and Complimentary Close
Baptist Christian (church) Episcopalian Lutheran Methodist Presbyterian Quaker	The Reverend (full name) (Title), (name of Church) (local address) 00000	Dear Mr./Ms. (surname): Sincerely,

Roman Catholic Clergy

His Holiness The Pope
Apostolic Palace
00210 Vatican City

Your Holiness:
Your obedient
servant,

His Eminence
(given name)
Cardinal (surname)
Archbishop of (Diocese
(local address) 00000

Your Eminence:
(formal)
Dear Cardinal
(surname):
(informal)
Yours faithfully,

The Most Reverend
(full name)
Archbishop of (Diocese)
(local address) 00000

Your Excellency:
(formal)
Dear Archbishop
(surname):
(informal)
Yours faithfully,

321

Addressee	Address on Letter and Envelope	Salutation and Complimentary Close
Catholic Clergy Roman	The Most Reverend (full name) Bishop of (City) (local address) 00000	Your Excellency: (formal) Dear Bishop (surname): (informal) Yours faithfully,
Catholic Clergy Orthodox	His Holiness The Patriarch (local address) 00000	Your Holiness: Your obedient servant,

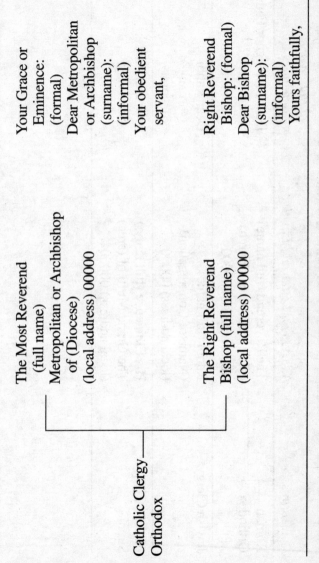

Catholic Clergy Orthodox		
The Most Reverend (full name) Metropolitan or Archbishop of (Diocese) (local address) 00000	Your Grace or Eminence: (formal) Dear Metropolitan or Archbishop (surname): (informal)	Your obedient servant,
The Right Reverend Bishop (full name) (local address) 00000	Right Reverend Bishop: (formal) Dear Bishop (surname): (informal)	Yours faithfully,

Addressee	Address on Letter and Envelope	Salutation and Complimentary Close
Roman ⌐ Orthodox ⌐	The Reverend (full name) (Title), (name of Church) (local address) 00000	Dear Monsignor/Father (surname): Yours sincerely,
Jewish Clergy	Rabbi (full name) (Name of Congregation) (local address) 00000	Dear Rabbi (surname): Sincerely,
Islamic Clergy Sunni	His Eminence (full name) The Grand Mufti of (area) (local address) 00000	Your Eminence: Sincerely,

Shiite

His Eminence (full name)
The Ayatollah of (area)
(local address) 00000

Your Eminence:
    Sincerely,

Sunni
Shiite

Imam (full name)
(name of mosque)
(local address) 00000

Imam (surname):
    Sincerely,

325

INDEX